NATURAL PROCESS ANALYSIS

(NPA): A Procedure for Phonological Analysis of Continuous Speech Samples

Wiley Series on Communication Disorders

Thomas J. Hixon, Advisory Editor

This collection of books has been developed by John Wiley & Sons to meet some of the needs in the field of communication disorders. The collection includes books on both normal and disordered speech, hearing, and language function. The authors of the collection have been selected because they are scientific and clinical leaders in their field and, we believe, are eminently qualified to make significant and scholarly contributions to the professional literature.

Language Development and Language Disorders
Lois Bloom and Margaret Lahey

Readings in Language Development
Lois Bloom

Readings in Childhood Language Disorders
Margaret Lahey

Elements of Hearing Science: A Programmed Text
Arnold M. Small

Natural Process Analysis (NPA):
A Procedure For Phonological Analysis
of Continuous Speech Samples
Lawrence D. Shriberg and Joan Kwiatkowski

ERRATUM

We apologize for an error which resulted in the omission of an important paragraph.

On page 39, under PROCEDURE for Final Consonant Deletion, insert the following as the first paragraph:

> Inspect all words in the VC and CVC columns. Include also words in Column 4, $C^n V(C)$ that end in a consonant only if the initial cluster was said correctly.

NATURAL PROCESS ANALYSIS

(NPA): A Procedure for Phonological Analysis of Continuous Speech Samples

Lawrence D. Shriberg
Joan Kwiatkowski
Department of Communicative Disorders
University of Wisconsin, Madison

John Wiley & Sons
New York • Chichester • Brisbane • Toronto

Library of Congress Catalog Card Number 80-51707
ISBN 0-471-07893-x

Printed in the United States of America

10 9 8 7 6 5 4 3 2 1

Foreword

For those who have struggled with the problems of systematizing their observations and conclusions about children with delayed speech and language, this contribution by Shriberg and Kwiatkowski will be eagerly received. Presented here is a strong argument for natural process analysis of such children and a practical, tested procedure for carrying out the analysis. In admirable fashion, *Natural Process Analysis (NPA): A Procedure for Phonological Analysis of Continuous Speech Samples* carefully leads the reader from the theoretical bases for the procedure, through the development of the clinical skills needed to carry out the analysis, to its vivid applications in case study examples. The hallmarks of this contribution are its thoroughness and timeliness. Importantly, it crosses traditional boundaries where linguistics, psycholinguistics, and speech-language pathology interface. All who read this contribution will realize that these materials are on the cutting-edge of research efforts to understand the problems of children with delayed speech and language. It is clear in this work that the procedure has evolved from a continuously moving research program that already has had many significant clinical payoffs for children with problems of speech-language delay.

Thomas J. Hixon
Advisory Editor in Communication Disorders

Contents

List of Tables

Table

PART I

Development of the Procedure

Introductory Concepts

A basic problem for phonologists is to account for *sound change*. This cover term encompasses all changes in the production of sounds, such as those that occur: in a language over time; when one dialect comes in contact with another; under different speaking conditions; as slips of the tongue; as a child acquires speech; and in other phonological domains. To account for sound change, phonologists must deal with sounds at an abstract, underlying level of representation, and at the manifest or surface level of speech production. Behavior at each level, and events that assumedly transpire between the underlying representation and the surface form are described by means of two concepts, *rules* and *processes*. Some phonologists use these two terms interchangeably; others have differentiated them quite differently than the distinctions we propose here.

Phonological *rules* describe information about constraints on word making and on sound making. Phonological rules capture this information about these constraints as they are observed in a language or in an individual speakers. In English, for example, observations such as (1) words may not begin with /ŋ/, (2) vowels are longer before final voiced obstruents than before voiceless obstruents, or (3) Scotty always says [t/s], also may be stated as rules. When stated as rules, however, using whatever formal symbolization the linguist finds convenient, they are no more explanatory than when stated less formally. Phonological rules simply describe observed regularity in behavior. Rules provide the phonologist a means for organizing, analyzing, and discussing phonological data.

The term *natural process* moves beyond description to an explanatory-level account of sound change. To use a previous example, /s/→[t] may be listed as an obligatory phonological *rule* for a child. It is a formal way of describing the fact that /s/ "changes to" [t] whenever /s/ at the underlying level is supposed to occur at the surface level. This same observation might also be proposed as an instance of the natural phonological *process* of Stopping. In the latter case, /s/→[t] purportedly is *explained* by a natural process that changes fricatives to stops. Such a sound change is viewed as a natural process if it satisfies two conditions: (1) a more complex articulatory structure at the underlying level is changed to a less complex structure at the surface level, and (2) the process is attested in a sufficient number of sound change phenomena in natural languages of the world. In the absence of a widely accepted measure of complexity, what constitutes a change from a more to a less complex structure is open to discussion. For example, a CCVC morpheme said as a CVC, has apparently been simplified; however, an /r/ said as a [w] is less obviously "simplified." Similarly, the number and type of sound change phenomena required to document a process as widely distributed, and hence natural, is a matter for linguists to deliberate.

Not surprisingly, the theoretical status of natural processes has been the subject of lively dialogue (Kenstowicz & Kisseberth, 1977; Sommerstein, 1977). Some phonologists, notably Stampe (1973) and Miller-Donnegan (1972) have been early and persistent proponents of an innateness view. They view the phonological system of a language as "the residue of an innate system of phonological processes, revised in certain ways by linguistic experiences" (Stampe, 1969, p. 443). Just what underlies this innate system is the matter to be resolved. Most phonologists (for example, Ohala, 1974; Oller, 1975; Foley, 1977; Locke, 1978) reject mentalistic concepts of innateness in favor of a view of natural processes that stresses their relationship to structural and physiological aspects of speech production.

Table 1 is an alphabetical list of only some of the sound changes that have been proposed as natural processes in a representative sample of the child phonology literature. This list is suggestive, not exhaustive. Many more terms and permutations of terms have been used to describe sound changes in child phonology. Three problems with this list are noted briefly; each will need to be addressed in context later.

First, many of these putative natural processes do not satisfy the dual criteria of accomplishing simplification and of being widely attested in synchronic and diachronic linguistics.* A sound change such as Final Consonant Deletion, for example, might satisfy both conditions, but Lateralization would be difficult to support as "natural." Second, some processes rival each other as explanations for a given sound change. Particularly as words become longer, the linguistic task of attributing a sound change to one process among several possibilities involves arbitrary theoretical conventions. Finally, the processes differ markedly in the extensiveness of underlying segments involved and in the variety of sound change outcomes. Cluster Reduction, for example, includes groups of related processes that have the same basic functions—the term encompasses all clusters and several types of sound change outcomes. In contrast, for example, Velar Fronting in English phonology is concerned only with changes of /k/ and /g/.

These considerations notwithstanding, the natural process as a linguistic unit has been used productively in many contemporary studies of normal phonological development (for example, Compton & Streeter, 1977; Schwartz & Folger, 1977; Klein, 1978) and this approach continues. Processes capture similarities in otherwise dissimilar surface behaviors. For example, a child's "substitutions" of [gɔgɪ] for "doggie" [g/d] and [tɛləvɪvən] for "television" [v/ʒ] share few phonetic features at the surface level. Process analysis, however, might view both sound changes as resulting from Assimilation. Processes assumedly are triggered by complex articulatory demands. They are phonological simplifications that occur reliably under certain morpheme structure conditions for certain children.

For clinical needs too, processes may have the conceptual and methodological adequacy that to date, neither segmental analyses (Powers, 1971), structural analyses (Faircloth & Dickerson, 1977), featural analyses (McReynolds & Engmann, 1975; Weiner & Bernthal, 1978), or generative phonological analyses (Compton, 1970; 1975) have been able to achieve. In the previous example, children with delayed speech who simplify by Assimilation may have other characteristics in common that are of interest for issues in theory and practice. Later in this text (see Part III: Guidelines for Interpretation and Additional Analyses) we present a detailed discussion of sound change phenomena in children's speech. Continuing here, the next section recounts the reasoning and the data base from which we developed a procedure for natural processes analysis for children with delayed speech.

---

* Synchronic linguistics examines data taken within a particular point in time; diachronic linguistics compares data from different points in time.

Table 1   Representative types of sound changes that have been described as natural processes in the child phonology literature

Absorption	Dissimilation
Aspiration	Frication (of stops, of
Assibilation	alveolars)
Assimilation (back, front)	Fronting (of velars, of
Bleaching	palatals)
Cluster Reduction	Glide loss
Coalescence	Gliding
Deaspiration	Glottal Replacement
Delateralization	Harmony (consonant H.,
Deletion (initial consonants,	vowel H.)
final consonants, unstressed	Labialization
syllables, stridents, liquids,	Labiovelarization
etc.)	Lateralization
Denasalization	Liquid Simplification
Dentalization	Liquidation
Deretroflexion	Loss of Coronality
Devoicing	Methathesis
Diminutive	Nasal Intrusion
Nasal Preference	Vocalization
Nasalization	Voicing
Neutralization	Vowel Adjustment
Raising	Vowel Epenthesis
Reduplication	Vowel Rounding
Stopping	Weakening (of stops, of
Strengthening	labials)

Alternative Approaches to Natural Process Analysis

Use of Articulation Tests for Natural Process Analysis

Despite perennial critique of commercially available articulation tests (Dubois & Bernthal, 1978; Faircloth & Faircloth, 1970; Ingram, 1976; Noll, 1970; Shriberg, 1978; 1980; Winitz, 1969), they continue to be the most often used clinical procedure for sampling speech. Because articulation tests do provide a rapid and controlled means of obtaining speech samples from young children, we first inspected their suitability as stimuli for natural process analysis.

Morpheme Structure
Constraints

One important characteristic of stimuli (words) to be used for natural process analysis is their structural complexity (canonical form).* As just introduced, natural processes are defined as simplifications affecting the surface level in response to demands posed by complex target sounds and canonical structures at the underlying, representational level. What sorts of demands on children are made by items on articulation tests?

Table 2 is a percentage analysis of the canonical forms of test items used in five articulation tests. Each of these tests was in use in one university speech-language and hearing clinic. Only items that test singleton consonants were tabulated for each test. For comparison, percentage of occurrence data are presented for the canonical forms used in continuous speech samples of 10 children with severely delayed speech whom we have been following in a longitudinal study. To make the appropriate comparison, only first occurrences of each lexical item in each sample rather than all words in each sample were tabulated. These data indicate that articulation test items make rather severe demands on children. Whereas 83 percent of the canonical forms used by children in continuous speech are one of the six simple shapes listed in Table 2, these forms are used in only 56 to 71 percent of the articulation test items. The remaining 29 to 44 percent of articulation test items have more complex canonical forms, including both more complex syllable shapes and more syllables per word. For young children with delayed speech, the complexity of some articulation test items may trigger simplification processes.

Data summarized in Table 3 suggest that simplification demands of articulation test items may be differentially weighted across sound classes. The singleton items on the five articulation tests were dichotomized into "simple" versus "complex" canonical forms (see Table 3) and percentaged for each sound class by target position. Stops tend

Table 2 Canonical forms in continuous speech samples attempted by 10 children with delayed speech compared to the canonical forms used in five articulation tests

| | Samples of Delayed Speech | | Articulation Tests | | | | |
| | Shriberg and Kwiatkowski (1977)[a] | | Hejna (1955) 64 items (%) | Goldman–Fristoe (1969) 42 items (%) | Pendergast et al. (1969) 67 items (%) | Templin–Darley (1969) 57 items (%) | Fisher–Logemann (1971) 70 items (%) |
Canonical Form	Mean Percent	Standard Deviation					
CVC	41.8	4.3	35.9	31.0	38.8	43.9	42.9
CV	18.6	4.2	1.6	0.0	3.0	3.5	1.4
VC	11.5	5.0	0.0	0.0	1.5	0.0	1.4
CVCV	5.3	2.7	9.4	9.5	10.4	3.5	15.7
CVCC	3.3	1.4	6.3	4.8	6.0	5.3	5.7
CCVC	2.5	3.6	3.1	11.9	3.0	8.8	4.3
	—	—	—	—	—	—	—
Percent accounted for	83		56	57	63	65	71
Percent not accounted for	17		44	43	37	35	29

[a] Based on total number of different words in each of 10 speech samples. Sample sizes ranged from 48−391 total words (mean of 220 words); number of different words per sample ranged from 30−102 words (mean of 76 words).

* The term *syllable form* (or *syllable shape*) is often confused with the term *canonical form* (or *canonical shape*). Syllable form describes the sequence of consonants and vowels within the syllable, for example, CVC, CCVC, whereas canonical form describes the sequence of syllables as they combine to form a word, for example, VCCVC. In monosyllabic words, therefore, syllable shape and canonical shape are identical.

Table 3 Percentage of simple canonical forms used in five articulation tests arranged by position of target sound in the word and sound class

Position of Target Sound in Word	Simple Canonical Form	Percentage of Simple Canonical Forms			
		Stops (6)	Nasals (3)	Fricative–Affricates (11)	Liquids–Glides (4)
Initial	CV(C)	77	40	50	35
Medial	CVCV(C)	88	83	47	26
Final	(C)VC	80	60	61	89

to be tested in simple shapes in all three target positions. Fricatives, affricates, liquids, and glides, however, are less often tested in simple canonical forms particularly in initial and medial target positions in words. Hence, sounds most likely to be in error in young children—fricatives, affricates, and liquids—are often "tested" in words that are likely to evoke a simplification process. Considering that an articulation test is supposed to yield information on a child's ability to articulate *sounds* (that is, a phonetic inventory), the use of words with complex canonical forms biases these data.

Syntactic, Morphophonemic, and Pragmatic Constraints

The requirement that articulation test words be picturable and readily identifiable places severe constraints on their syntactic form. Of the 300 singleton words tested on the five articulation tests, 92 percent are nouns (across individual tests the range was from 90 to 97 percent). In comparison, our studies indicate that nouns comprise only 24 percent of the parts of speech used by normal five-year olds (see also Templin, 1957). This disproportionate weighting of nouns on articulation tests could affect speech performance data. A preliminary study of three children with delayed speech indicated that final clusters in nouns were more often reduced than initial clusters in nouns. Just the opposite was observed for verbs; initial clusters were more often reduced than final clusters. Recent studies support these data. Paul and Shriberg (1979) have found evidence for syntactic and morphophonemic factors affecting children's use of natural processes; Campbell and Shriberg (1979) have found evidence that pragmatic factors influence children's use of natural processes.

The point here is that articulation tests generally are insensitive to what is properly the phonological domain. Missing from the articulation test situation are precisely those elements of continuous speech (language factors) that influence a child's phonological production. Our position is that accurate assessment and differential management strategies require *thorough* description of the child's phonological system.

It is of interest to complete this section with some additional information on the articulation tests we sampled. Each of the five articulation tests also contained the following percentages of inflected nouns on singleton items: Pendergast et al., 19.4 percent; Templin–Darley, 14 percent; Hejna, 10.9 percent; Fisher–Logemann, 10 percent; and Goldman–Fristoe, 4.8 percent. These inflections were mostly plural markers. The magnitude of these percentages is significant considering that decisions about a child's "mastery of a sound" may be based on performance on only one to three articulation test items. Plural inflections tax the child's phonological system in two ways: they add a morphophonemic component to performance and they may also add a word-final cluster to the canonical form (bike, bikes; CVC, CVCC) or add a syllable (match, matches; CVC, CVCVC). To the extent that syntactic forms and morphophonemic markers constrain performance, speech sound mastery data from articulation tests may be confounded.

Mode of Elicitation Constraints

Our exploration of the suitability of articulation test data as input to natural process analyses includes several analyses of a longitudinal sample of children with delayed speech. Ten children with severe speech delays at the beginning of the study have been tested twice each year since 1975. The protocol includes an articulation test (the *Photo Articulation Test,* Pendergast et al., 1969) given both by spontaneous and imitative modes, and a lengthy continuous speech sample.

Inspection of the first two years' data has been undertaken to compare the frequency of process usage on the articulation test when given spontaneously versus by imitation. Unsystematic differences across processes and children are evident. Some processes are more frequent for some children in imitation, and some processes are more frequent when elicited spontaneously. Garnica and Edwards (1977) and Leonard et al. (in press) have examined related complexities in studies of young children with normally developing speech. Moreover, there is little concordance in the frequency of process usage when derived from articulation test responses versus continuous speech samples.

Like other language variables (Barrie-Blackley, Musselwhite, & Rogister, 1978; Bloom & Lahey, 1978), phonological processes appear to be sensitive to complex linguistic and extralinguistic factors associated with mode of elicitation. Our examination of articulation test data as a potential base for natural process analysis was undertaken with the hope that a word-list approach could be productive. Perhaps such citation-form testing (Ladefoged, 1975) may continue to be useful for assessing articulatory distortions and the residual articulation errors of older children. For natural process analysis of the speech of young children with delayed speech, however, the results of our studies mandate an alternative approach.

Use of a Nonsense Word Task for Natural Process Analysis

A brief account of our second series of studies is of archival interest for comparison to other procedures for natural process analyses that have begun to appear (Compton, 1978; McReynolds & Elbert, 1978; Weiner, 1978). Because nonsense words possess attractive control characteristics (they are free of lexical bias, they can be controlled for length, canonical structure, and segment type and sequence), we studied the reliability, efficiency, and validity of a nonsense word task for natural process analysis. In 1976, we developed a 76-item task in which each of 14 phonological processes was tested by means of a delayed imitation paradigm (for example, "This is a *big* [ik]—This is a *little* _____"). Nonsense word "creatures" were constructed with the potential to trigger only one process. For example, "This is a sitting [lɑ]—This is a walking _____", might trigger Liquid Simplification. A checklist procedure allowed nonambiguous scoring of the 14 processes and each process received a percentage score.

After determining that preschool children with normal phonological development could perform adequately on the nonsense syllable task, we obtained several continuous speech samples and nonsense word task results from a group of 12 preschool children with delayed speech development. The nonsense word task had adequate test-retest stability for most of the 14 processes and the scoring procedures yielded adequate interjudge agreement. But, the procedure did not demonstrate adequate concurrent validity. Spearman Rho correlations calculated for the frequency of process usage in continuous speech compared to that obtained from the nonsense word task were only low-to-moderate and statistically nonsignificant. As with the articulation test/continuous speech comparisons just discussed, some processes were more often used in the continuous speech samples, while others had higher percentages in the nonsense syllable task. Item analyses were not productive; we could find no consistent trends at lower levels of the data. Subsequent adjustments in items to account for memory constraints on the delayed elicitation procedure failed to resolve relevant problems.

Taken together with evidence from our studies of articulation tests, the implications of these data seem clear: *natural process analysis is best based on a sample of continuous speech.* Procedures that involve responses to a word list evoked spontaneously or by immediate or delayed imitation (for example, Compton, 1975; Weiner, 1978), yield unstable data. In addition to providing a valid sample base for process analysis, a continuous speech sample has the richest potential for integrated analyses of speech-language data, as we illustrate later in this text.

Development of a Procedure for Natural Process Analysis of Continuous Speech

Part II of this text is an instructional package for a procedure for Natural Process Analysis of continuous speech samples (hereafter, NPA). Here, we review rationale and data for the major technical problems that required resolution as the procedure was developed. All other procedural details are fully addressed in the instructional package.

Choice of Processes for Inclusion in NPA

From among the many sound changes described in the literature (see Table 1), NPA includes only the following eight processes: Final Consonant Deletion, Velar Fronting, Stopping, Palatal Fronting, Liquid Simplification, Regressive and Progressive Assimilation, Cluster Reduction, and Unstressed Syllable Deletion. Inclusion of only these processes is based on the outcomes of three questions we asked of the candidates we inspected.

1. Is this sound change reasonably a natural process?

2. Is this natural process seen frequently in preschool and school aged children with delayed speech?

3. Can this process be scored reliably by speech-language pathologists?

Criterial judgments in answer to each of these questions evolved from analyses of data obtained during the studies just reviewed, from additional analyses of speech samples from our tape library, and from review of current dialogue in the phonology literature.

After sorting the processes into nonduplicative labels, we first inspected the question of *naturalness,* using the dual criteria discussed earlier on page 3. To qualify as a natural process, a sound change must satisfy two conditions: the sound change must accomplish simplification and the sound change must be widely attested in natural language data. These two requisites for viewing a sound change as a natural process warrant careful examination.

We take the position that only phonemic *deletions* and phonemic *substitutions* (replacements) qualify as simplifications of underlying forms.* Phonemic *distortions* (approximations), in contrast, are viewed as lower-level phenomena that reflect articulatory imprecision. As far as we can determine, this particular view of what is properly a *natural process* is unique to our laboratory. It is, however, the only position that we believe is correct in the context of clinical speech pathology. This view limits phonological simplification to only those sounds that are phonemic in the child's language. Hence, "distortions" of sounds, such as dentalization, lateralization, or palatalization of fricatives are ascribed to lower-level, articulatory processes.

Our reasoning for limiting the term *natural process* to only those sound changes that involve deletion or replacement of sounds that are phonemic in a child's language stems from several types of observations. First, we wish to keep distinct, those aspects of normal speech sound acquisition in a child that are due to cognitive-linguistic development from those due to sensory-motor development. Behaviors that are described for each domain of development are generally divided into phonological versus phonetic, respectively. For example, children *attempt* /s/ targets within their first fifty morphemes (Ferguson & Farwell, 1975), (phonological), but it may take them a long time before /s/ is said correctly as [s], rather than [ş] (phonetic). Children's phonetic development proceeds gradually as sensory-motor control approaches adult values (Anthony, et al., 1971; Kent, 1976). Phonological knowledge proceeds gradually, also, but knowledge of the phonemes of one's language precedes articulatory precision (see Kent, 1976, for a review of acoustic data that indicate that adult values on some articulatory parameters are not reached until 11 years). For these reasons, we think that it is incorrect to ascribe to a phonological simplification realm, sound change that can be readily and adequately understood as articulatory imprecision.

A second observation that has influenced our views about distortions concerns linguistic processing errors in adults, commonly called "slips of the tongue." Studies of these sound changes indicate that they involve *metathesis* (transposition) and *assimilations,* as well as substitutions, such as those associated with Stopping and Fronting (Fromkin, 1973). Adult speakers are not likely, however, to suddenly dentalize a sound, [z̪], or derhotacize a sound, [ɹ]. Such distortions by a normal speaker, in fact, are associated only with temporary sensory-motor deficits, such as those that might occur following dental anesthesia, intoxication, or extreme fatigue.

This conceptual distinction between distortions and deletions/substitutions is fundamental to NPA procedures, and is especially important when attempting to diagnose the origin of the speech delay and plan an intervention approach. These matters are described in detail in Part III of the text. Note also that this conceptual distinction necessitates particular care in phonetic transcription of speech errors. For example, [w/r] is coded as a natural process sound change (Liquid Simplification), whereas [ɹ/r] (derhotacized) is annotated as a distortion.

To assess processes on the second criteria for inclusion, our working papers have yielded ample data on the frequency of occurrence of processes in children with moderately to severely delayed speech. Processes such as Reduplication, for example, have been well documented in young children (Ingram, 1976), but Reduplication is not prevalent in our speech samples. Several other processes occurred only infrequently in the samples; the eight processes retained were the only processes that occurred consis-

---

* If the child has the sound correct anywhere in the phonetic inventory (see page 45) and passes appropriate minimal-pairs discrimination testing, we assume that the child's underlying forms are essentially adultlike. Recent discussion among child phonologists is especially controversial on the evidential requirements for this assumption (Macken, 1978b; Smith, 1978; Weismer, Dinnsen, and Elbert, 1979).

tently in our studies. Unstressed Syllable Deletion is the least prevalent of the eight processes, but children with severely delayed speech demonstrate syllable deletions often enough to warrant its retention. Division of this process into two-syllable word deletions and three-plus syllable word deletions was motivated by data from our speech samples. Clearly, children deleted unstressed syllables in three-plus syllable words significantly more often than they deleted unstressed syllables in two-syllable words.

Finally, the criterion of transcription reliability warrants comment. Our previous work in teaching clinicians to transcribe articulation errors (Shriberg, 1972; Shriberg & Swisher, 1972) suggested that issues in phonetic transcription would be important to address. In the course of studies leading to a finalized NPA procedure, one potential process in particular, required careful study: voicing differences. The literature on historical sound change provides ample data on sound changes involving voicing differences; specifically, Prevocalic Voicing and Postvocalic Devoicing (Stampe, 1973). However, our experience indicates that phonetic transcription of voicing differences is extremely unreliable (Shriberg & Kent, in preparation). For example, to discriminate reliably, devoicing [d̥], [z̥], [d̥ʒ]) from cognate substitutions ([t/d], [s/z], [tʃ/dʒ]) requires considerable training and even with training is difficult to retain. At best, such decisions have marginal reliability.

Because of the difficulty in transcribing reliably all voicing features, we elect to treat all voicing differences, including supposed cognate substitutions, as articulatory distortions. That is, although sound changes involving partial voicing or partial devoicing would be excluded as a "natural" process because they are *distortions*, cognate *substitutions* (for example [t/d]) would satisfy the criteria of naturalness as developed here. Because of the reliability-of-transcription problem, however, voicing processes have been excluded from NPA procedures. In support of this decision we do note that: (1) adultlike stability of voicing control may not be reached normally until about eight years of age (Kent, 1976), (2) voicing contrasts may be actually indeterminent acoustically for some children seen clinically (Costley & Broen, 1976; Peters & Lauffer, 1976), and (3) as suggested in one of our studies, voicing errors in young children may contribute little if any to intelligibility ratings. Along with other sound change data that does not get coded as a natural process, all observed changes in voicing are annotated in the appropriate place in the *Summary* section of the procedure to follow and are used in differential diagnosis.

Decision To Attribute a Sound Change to Only One Process

Linguists have long debated the problem of rule (or process) ordering in deriving surface forms from underlying forms (Anderson, 1974; Hooper, 1976; Kiparsky, 1968; Koutsoudas, Sanders, & Noll, 1974). In child phonology, rule-ordered derivations typically have been proposed to "explain" surface forms for children. For example, Ingram (1976) discusses the following proposed derivation for the word "lamb" said by a child as [b̥ap]:

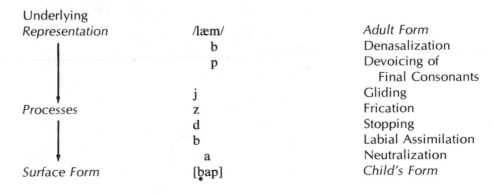

Underlying Representation	/læm/	Adult Form
	b	Denasalization
	p	Devoicing of Final Consonants
	j	Gliding
Processes	z	Frication
	d	Stopping
	b	Labial Assimilation
	a	Neutralization
Surface Form	[b̥ap]	Child's Form

Notice here that the vowel change involves only one process; the final consonant change presumes the operations of two processes; and the initial consonant change assumes participation of no less than four processes, ordered relative to each other and relative to the two processes for the final consonant. In an insightful discussion of such derivations, Menn (1978) notes that rewrite rules can be made to handle such phenomena but only by "brute force."

Aside from the problematic theoretical issues, rule-ordered derivations of speech errors are inadmissable for clinical needs. Sound change analyses that depend on the linguistic intuitions of the examiner have little chance of widespread utility (Shriberg & Kwiatkowski, 1977). Our solution has been to place restrictions on the stimuli used for process analysis and to develop conventions that attribute sound change to only one process.*

First, we restrict process coding to monosyllable words (except of course, for Unstressed Syllable Deletion). This decision preserves approximately 75 percent of the data in free speech samples (Roberts, 1965). In light of normative information on Stage III, *Phonology of the Simple Morphemes* (see Appendix A), assessing processes in simple morphemes is appropriate. As described later in the case studies, polysyllabic words remain available for inspection, once processes in monosyllabic words have been well defined.†

The second procedural strategy was to develop a sequence for process coding of the monosyllabic words. Inspection of our speech samples indicated clearly that some processes are more likely than others to account for a given sound change. For example, a change of [d/g] in [dɛt] for "get" is more likely to be accounted for by Velar Fronting than by Regressive Assimilation. Children who produce such sound change will invariably show Velar Fronting in some nonambiguous situation (for example, [d/k] in [di] for "key"), but will not generally show Regressive Assimilation unambiguously. After discovery of several implicational relationships such as these, and in consideration of other phonological literature, we determined a hierarchical structure for process coding. Each sound change is attributed to only one process and processes are coded in a fixed sequence. Attributing a sound change to *two* processes is allowed only in one case, that in which a word-final consonant assimilates to a word-initial consonant before the word-final consonant is deleted. In [mæ] for "pan," for example, the initial consonant sound change is coded as Regressive Assimilation (because the nasal feature of the final consonant has assimilated to the initial consonant, and the final consonant deletion is coded as Final Consonant Deletion). Admittedly, this one exception to the rule disallowing ordered processes is arbitrary. It is the one concession to mainstream phonology that seems warranted empirically and acceptable technically.

---

* M. L. Edwards (personal communication) disagrees with our view of rule-ordered derivations; her comments are instructive.

> Processes are not arbitrarily formulated or contrived and put in a particular order just to account for the surface forms of a particular word. There is, or should be, independent evidence for each of the processes, that is, they should be attested in other words. Ordered derivations make predictions about the forms that a word may appear in and may go through (diachronically) as the child progresses. Moreover, the concept of ordered derivations has implications for remediation. The process ordered later in the derivation are managed first. For example, if final /m,p,b/ are neutralized to [p], then final devoicing would be worked on before denasalization.

We concur with Edwards' view of the *potential* utility of rule-ordered derivations. Our reservations, however, concern (1) the lack of diachronic data on children with speech sound delays that would support a parallel between rule-ordered derivations and the sequence of changes in word forms, (2) the ability of linguists or clinicians readily to find independent evidence in a corpus for each process in a derivation, and (3) the problem in establishing reliable ways to choose among several possible process orderings, so as to know which process was truly last in a derivation.

† P. L. Porter, in an unpublished working paper completed after this text was set, provides evidence that polysyllable words can be analyzed by means of a modified NPA procedure. Her data suggest that a child will use the same processes in polysyllable words that he or she is currently using in monosyllable words.

Type versus Token Coding of the Continuous Speech Data

A decision had to be made as to whether to use only some arbitrary number of intelligible words in the sample (tokens) or only an arbitrary number of different words (types). Several of our studies and data from Templin (1957) indicate that the percentages each procedure (token versus type) yields for parts of speech and for morpheme structures are essentially similar. Transcription and sequential coding of an arbitrary number of tokens is faster, but the data are less generalizable. That is, token procedures are biased by repetitions of particular lexical items that occur frequently in the sample. Our decision is to use only the first occurrence (type) of each word. A conversational speech sample of approximately 225 intelligible (glossable) words will yield approximately 40 percent (90) different words for natural process analyses. Longer samples will yield more words, but the percentage of new words (type/token ratio) decreases with sample length. Importantly, the remaining 60 percent of the data—all subsequent occurrences of each word—are available in the transcription for a variety of additional analyses described in the instructional package. Faircloth and Dickerson (1977) also suggest that a 90-word sample is necessary and sufficient for their conversational speech analyses procedure for children with severely delayed speech.

Reliability, Efficiency, and Validity Studies

As is apparent in the instructional package to follow, this procedure for natural process analysis requires considerable attention to detail and adherence to many seemingly arbitrary conventions. Because it does require an investment of time to learn the procedures and to accomplish an NPA with each child, data on its reliability, efficiency, and validity are important to establish. Rather than relegate this information to an appendix, we have positioned it to be read here.

Reliability of the Procedure

The term *reliability* refers to several characteristics or properties expected of a procedure. For NPA data, one important property is *sample stability*. If we test different children with the same set of stimuli, the linguistic data that are obtained should be structurally comparable, that is, structurally stable. Moreover, samples of the same child's speech obtained on different occasions should be temporally stable.

In addition to these two forms of sample stability, another required characteristic of NPA data is that they be based on reliable procedural activities by clinicians. There should be substantial agreement between a clinician's analyses of the same data when done on two separate occasions *(intrajudge agreement)*. Moreover, there should be substantial agreement between analyses of a sample done by prospective users of a procedure and by someone who assumedly is competent in the procedure *(interjudge agreement)*.

Several studies of *sample stability* and *intra/interjudge agreement* have assessed the reliability of NPA data.

Sample Stability Studies

Structural Stability

Structural stability of NPA data has been assessed in several studies: representative data are presented in Table 4. Each of the twelve children whose NPA data are presented in Table 4 had moderately to severely delayed speech. Their ages range from four years to seven and one-half years, with a mean of five years, eight months. Some children also had moderate cognitive and/or language delays, but they did not have gross intellectual, structural, or neurogenic deficits. Of interest in this table here, are only the first two

Table 4 Descriptive statistics for Natural Process Analysis (NPA) from continuous speech samples. The 12 children had moderately to severely delayed speech

Subjects Variable: Age	1 4-0	2 4-0	3 4-5	4 5-4	5 5-4	6 5-10	7 5-10	8 6-1	9 6-2	10 7-2	11 7-5	12 7-6	Mean	Standard Deviation
Type/Token Ratios														
Total intelligible words	252	246	224	199	264	278	221	107	223	260	194	263	228	46
Total words coded	72	80	85	91	71	96	116	52	77	105	80	69	83	17
Percent word coded	29	33	38	46	27	35	52	48	35	40	41	26	38	8
Total monosyllable words	221	205	185	163	233	237	173	95	198	190	166	229	191	40
Total monosyllable words coded	54	55	61	67	58	67	83	44	61	71	60	53	61	10
Percent monosyllable words coded	24	27	33	41	25	28	48	46	31	37	36	23	33	8
Total polysyllable words	31	41	39	36	31	41	48	12	25	70	28	34	36	14
Total polysyllable words coded	18	25	24	25	23	29	33	8	16	34	20	16	23	8
Percent polysyllable words coded	58	61	62	69	74	71	69	67	64	49	71	47	64	9
Parts of Speech[a]														
Percent nouns	27.8	30.0	30.6	24.2	19.7	32.3	28.4	36.5	22.0	34.3	28.8	39.1	29.5	5.7
Percent verbs	23.6	28.8	30.6	18.7	23.9	22.9	31.9	15.4	23.4	34.3	23.8	23.1	25.0	5.5
Percent adjectives	8.3	6.3	8.2	8.8	7.0	7.3	4.3	15.4	10.4	7.6	10.0	11.6	8.8	2.9
Percent adverbs	8.3	5.0	10.6	6.6	7.0	13.5	3.4	11.5	13.0	7.6	5.0	4.3	8.0	3.4
Percent pronouns	8.3	11.3	8.2	9.9	11.2	4.2	6.0	1.9	7.8	2.9	8.8	2.9	7.0	3.3
Percent prepositions	6.9	6.3	4.7	6.6	11.2	8.3	9.5	1.9	3.9	6.7	7.5	2.9	6.4	2.7
Natural Process Usage[b]														
Final Consonant Deletion	X	X	X		X	X	X	X		X	X	X		
Velar Fronting						X		X		X		X		
Stopping	X	X	X	X	X	X	X	X		X	X	X		
Palatal Fronting						X						X		
Liquid Simplification		X				X			X	X	X	X		
Assimilation		X	X			X	X		X	X	X			
Cluster Reduction	X	X	X	X	X	X	X	X	X	X	X	X		
Unstressed Syllable Deletion	X	X	X		X	X				X	X	X		

[a] The following were excluded from these tabulations: proper nouns, contractions, conjunctions, interjections, catenatives, and infinitives. Classification of parts of speech was determined by usage in context. Reference: Webster's *Seventh New Collegiate Dictionary*. Springfield, Mass.: Merriam, 1970.

[b] An "X" was given each process if it was observed for any target sound in any appropriate morpheme structure. In the original data summary process usage is coded for each appropriate target sound as "always," "sometimes," or "never" used in the sample corpus.

sectors—the type/token ratios for canonical structures and the parts of speech percentage data.

On examination, both the distributions of canonical structures and parts of speech usage data are similar across the twelve children (small standard deviations) and are remarkably similar to published normative data (Catterette & Jones, 1974; Templin, 1957; Wepman & Hass, 1969). Considering the range of age and language abilities of the children and the variety of topics that were discussed in the samples, NPA sampling procedures do seem to yield a structurally stable linguistic base for process analyses.

Temporal Stability

To assess the temporal stability of NPA data we obtained speech samples from a five-year-old boy with severely delayed speech. Sampling sessions were separated by 24 days. Stimuli used on both occasions (picture books) were comparable, but deliberately not identical. Sampling and subsequent analyses of these data on both occasions were accomplished by the same person (JK).

Comparison of the two data sets was accomplished by tabulating the number of exact agreements on the NPA Summary Sheet for each sampling session. Of the 80 items that were appropriate to inspect for this comparison, 56 (71 percent) agreed exactly on the two occasions. An additional 16 items (21 percent) did not agree because data available in one sample were not available in the other.* Considering that the wide array of processes this child used posed a maximally difficult test, these data suggest that NPA data are temporally stable; large scale studies are required for more fine-grained analyses.

Intra/Interjudge Agreement Studies

Intrajudge Agreement

Intrajudge reliability, agreement with oneself, has been assessed as follows. In association with a practicum in phonological disorders, six graduate students in communication disorders were given a brief overview of the NPA procedure and a preliminary manual of the procedures. Students were from different undergraduate training programs and their academic backgrounds and clinical experiences in phonological disorders varied considerably. Continuous speech samples of six children with moderately to severely delayed speech were obtained by one of the authors (JK). Each student completed a natural process analysis from an audio tape of one child; six weeks later each student completed a second analysis of the same tape. The speech samples were originally recorded on a Sony Model TC-92 portable cassette audio tape recorder with an external microphone on Sony low-noise audio cassette tape. Transcription was accomplished using Sony Model ER-740 booth recorders and Koss 747 headphones set at the most comfortable listening level for each clinician.

Across all clinicians and all children, approximately 83 percent of decisions made on the original analysis agreed with those made on the reanalysis six weeks later. Intrajudge disagreements were traced to two sources. First, as expected, a student's background and demonstrable skills in phonetic transcription are important determinants of intrajudge agreement. Many of the disagreements were due to at best, tenuous phonetic transcription skills. The procedure does not require a high level of skill in close transcription, but it does require that symbolization be used consistently.

The second source of disagreements was associated with instructional control at each stage of the procedure. Some disagreements were related to instructions that were incorrect, incomplete, or ambiguous. These problems have been corrected in successive versions of the procedures. Other disagreements were due to failure to follow

---

* Since this study was conducted we try to ensure that each sample will include all relevant data. Specifically, we have available, objects, pictures, and activites that will evoke words containing infrequent sounds such as /ʃ/, /ʒ/, /tʃ/, /dʒ/ (see Part II, Sampling).

directions, particularly those in which order of precedence of coding decisions is critical.

Each of these sources of disagreement has been addressed in the current version of the NPA procedure. Phonetic transcription conventions have been developed; they are described in the instructional package. And to ensure that all instructions are understood, the reader is provided with several ways to assess knowledge of the procedure, including some review/discussion questions following each subsection.

Interjudge Agreement
To assess how well NPA analyses by clinicians agree with analyses by an "expert," the following study was conducted.

Seven graduate students, including majors in speech, language, and hearing, were each provided with a tape recorded speech sample of a four-year-old child with severely delayed speech. The master tape had been recorded on a Uher Model 4000 reel-to-reel audio recorder on Scotch 171 audio tape. Seven audio cassettes (Sony low-noise) were dubbed simultaneously on a Sony audio laboratory system using Sony Model ER 740 booth recorders. Each student independently studied a preliminary version of the NPA procedures before completing an NPA analysis from his or her tape. To assess interjudge agreement under typical clinical conditions, students transcribed the tape using whatever cassette recorder they had access to. One of the authors (JK) completed an analysis of the child, using the original audio tape to ensure the best fidelity.

Analyses of the data were accomplished in the same manner as just described for sample stability. Of the 80 decision boxes on the NPA Summary Sheet that allow point-by-point comparison, how often did the seven students agree with the criterion "expert"? In 19 of the 24 decisions about the child's phonetic inventory (79 percent), at least five of the seven judges agreed with the criterion judge. The remaining 21 percent of the decisions in which less than five of the seven judges agreed with the criterion judge were readily explained by differences in transcription, by a failure to follow directions, and by some obviously careless errors in entering data. Percentage of agreement on the decisions about phonological processes were not independent of these errors. That is, depending on the specifics of the situation, disagreement in transcription may ensure that all subsequent coding decisions will differ. Keeping this in mind, five of the seven judges agreed with the criterion judge on over 50% of the remaining 56 boxes on the Summary Sheet.

These data on reliability of the NPA procedure support its sample stability and intra-interjudge reliability. For both characteristics, clinicians must be completely familiar with all aspects of the instructional package. These data presented here only approximate reliability coefficients that can be obtained with the present version of the procedure. The instructional package now contains several sections designed expressly to provide feedback on a reader's understanding of the procedures; we believe that clinicians should have completed several simulated analyses before completing an analyses for clinical purposes on a "real" child.

Efficiency of the Procedure

In each of the two studies with graduate students just discussed, time data (to the nearest five minutes) were kept on all phases of the analysis. These data are presented here, followed by a discussion of the clinical efficiency of NPA procedures.

During the intrajudge agreement study each of the six student clinicians kept track of the time it took to complete the second of the two NPA analyses. Times ranged from one and one-half to three and one-half hours. Total times for each of the three stages of analysis, Transcribing, Coding, and Summarizing, were associated with differences in the length of the sample, severity of the speech delay, and the student's experience in phonetic transcription.

In the study in which seven students each transcribed and analyzed the same tape of one child with severely delayed speech, the following data were obtained.

	Mean (Minutes)	Standard Deviation (Minutes)	Proportion of Total Time (%)	Words Per Minute
Transcription	155	72	43	0.7
Coding	128	30	36	1.3
Summary	76	21	21	8.4 (minutes per process)

We present these figures primarily for their value as reference points for a reader's first attempt at an NPA analysis. This was the first analysis attempted by these seven clinicians. Note that 43 percent of the total time was spent in phonetic transcription, which for the 210 words in the sample turned out to average only *0.7 words transcribed per minute!* Clinicians do improve their transcription skills with practice, which in turn, increases the rate of transcription. Moreover, with increasing familiarity with the instructional procedure, the rate of words coded per minute (1.3 in this study) can be increased. Similarly, the figure here of 8.4 minutes to complete operations needed to summarize the data on each of the eight natural processes becomes more efficient.

Clinicians who have had the opportunity to do several analyses have found that total times for completing analyses reduce with practice as follows. For a 200-word sample, times of approximately 50 minutes for transcription (or approximately four words per minute) and another 50 minutes for the remaining procedures have become average. Hence, for most speech-delayed children, a complete NPA analysis seems to require about one and one-half hours to accomplish. "Short-form" versions to answer only particular questions about a child's use of processes taken even less time.

Overall, these data are viewed as support for the NPA as a clinically efficient instrument. Contemporary language analysis procedures (Miller, 1980) require comparable amounts of time. If a continuous speech sample is to be used for both language analyses and speech analyses of the type described in Part II, Part III, and Part IV of this text, the time spent in sampling and transcription is particularly efficient. With appropriate adjustments in recording the data, the same continuous speech sample can be used for both purposes, thus ruling out the need for a special phonology "test" and providing the corpus for an integrated analysis of speech and language as illustrated in the case studies.

Validity of the Procedure

Does the NPA procedure *validly* assess natural processes? In the absence of a presumedly valid instrument to which NPA data can be compared, two types of validity have been addressed: construct validity and predictive validity.

Construct validity requires consensus that the eight processes included in the procedure are properly defined and that they comprise the proper domain of natural processes. Rationales that led to definition and selection of just these eight processes were presented earlier in this text. The data on use of natural processes in Table 4 (page 14) are viewed as lending construct validity to these conceptual and technical considerations. These eight natural processes are sensitive to individual differences in sound change patterns among the 12 children. Even at this summary level of data presentations, only two children (Subjects 2 and 11) use exactly the same processes. Marked individual differences in process usage are a consistent finding in studies of children with normal and delayed speech acquisition (Ferguson & Farwell, 1975; Shriberg & Kwiatkowski, 1977; in submission). These differences are more pronounced than the age-related, consistent patterns characteristic of segmental and featural analyses. We interpret this relative independence of processes from phonetic "mastery" constraints as support for viewing process usage as phonological phenomena, rather than lower-level articulatory phenomena. That is, although there seems to be developmental sequences to the dissolution of each process (see Appendix A), the inventories of processes used by children with delayed speech are highly individualized.

Predictive validity for the procedure has been established in our clinical management studies (Shriberg & Kwiatkowski, 1977; 1978; in submission) and is illustrated in the case studies presented in this text. A procedure gains predictive validity as the individual patterns of natural processes such as those presented in Table 4 are associated with diagnostic and management outcomes. Use of the NPA procedures for research in normal and delayed speech development is encouraging (Campbell & Shriberg, 1979; Paul & Shriberg, 1979; Shriberg & Smith, in submission). The procedures have begun to allow for an integrated analysis of children's language systems, including the role of the phonological component in differential diagnosis.*

Review and Discussion Questions†

<table>
<tr><td>Basic Concepts</td><td>

1. Define the following terms.

    a. Sound Change (3).

    b. Phonological rule (3).

    c. Natural process (3).

    d. Canonical form (6).

    e. Syllable form (6).

    f. Morphophonemic (7).

2. Describe several characteristics of articulation tests that limit their use in natural process analyses (6).

3. A nonsense-syllable task was found to yield invalid data for natural process analyses (8). Why might nonsense syllables be "processed" differently than real words?

</td></tr>
</table>

---

* Working papers in our project have used the NPA procedure to inspect phonological development and performance in persons with hearing impairment, intellectual deficits, and motor-speech involvement as causal-contributing factors to the speech delay.

† Numbers in parentheses refer to page numbers in text where discussion of each term/concept begins.

NPA Development

4. What three criteria were used to determine whether a phonological process would be included in NPA (9)?

5. Discuss the "naturalness" criteria used in NPA, in particular, the rationale for distinguishing between deletions/substitutions versus distortions. Do you agree with the position taken by the authors (9)?

6. What is a phonological derivation? Why are rule-ordered phonological derivations greatly restricted in NPA (11)?

7. What is a word *type;* a word *token?* Why are a minimum number of word *types* used in NPA (13)?

8. How can you, as a clinician, test the following?

   a. The *intrajudge* reliability of your NPA data (13).

   b. The *interjudge* reliability of your NPA data (13).

   c. The *temporal stability* of a child's NPA data (13).

PART II

Instructional Package for the NPA Procedure

Introduction

The procedure for natural process analysis (NPA) of continuous speech samples presented here includes five phases: Sampling, Recording, Transcribing, Coding, and Summarizing. The benefits gained from completing the operations at each phase must be weighed against costs in time to the clinician. For specific clinical applications, "short cuts" can be taken which improve efficiency. With practice, several operations within phases can be accomplished in one entry, rather than in the step-wise fashion presented here. Also, for some limited clinical applications, the Recording, Transcribing, and/or Coding phase can be bypassed entirely. For example, once the procedure is thoroughly learned, the clinician can fill out a Summary Sheet directly from a live or tape recorded speech sample. Because of the amount of detail, however, the procedures are best learned in the sequence described.

Sampling

Stimulus Conditions

Stimulus conditions for continuous speech samples should be thoroughly specified. As discussed in Miller (1980), many factors are important to control. Ideally, clinicians should be able to use one speech sample for analyses of all levels of the child's language, including phonology.

We make no claim that the stimulus conditions we use produce "representative" speech-language samples. In conjunction with the clinician behaviors described below, however, these stimulus conditions do yield samples suitable for natural process analyses for young children and even for children with severely unintelligible speech. We ask a child to do one or more of six things.

1. Describe activities depicted on sequence story cards.
2. Tell a story using pictures in a book.
3. Converse about interests and experiences.

4. Comment while engaged in play with familiar and unfamiliar toys.

5. Arrange small objects and figures (animals and people) and comment on each arrangement when finished (for example, "the man is sitting in a boat").

6. View a familiar story through a toy movie viewer and comment to the clinician on the observed actions and events (the clinician ostensibly does not know the story and can not view the movie).

For the purposes of language analyses, certain constraints on sampling must be observed which are not necessary if the sample is to serve only for a speech analysis. For all types of sampling, infrequent sounds such as [ʃ], [ʒ],* [tʃ], and [dʒ]* may not occur in the continuous speech sample unless objects or pictures are used to ensure that tokens for these sounds in CV, VC, or CVC words are evoked. Particularly if the sample is to provide a corpus for extensive analyses, the clinician must be sure that materials that will evoke these sounds are available.

Clinician Behaviors

Clinician behaviors serve two functions. First, they serve to evoke speech by use of open-ended questions and by structuring activities so that verbalization is a natural and meaningful part of the task. The search for topics of interest to the child should seem effortless and enjoyable. With very young or noncommunicative children, additional clinical antics may be necessary to prompt natural speech. Clinician models that include exaggerated intonation evoke the same from children (Shriberg, 1975; in press). Also, some children may speak too fast, requiring appropriate adjustments in sampling arrangements by the clinician. The clinician may need to ask the child (unobtrusively) to slow down so that the clinician can understand "all the child's ideas."

The second clinician task is to repeat, word for word, what the child *intended to say*. This task (called *glossing*) is critical for subsequent transcription from an audio tape. Children will adapt to such behavior if the repetitions appear to be motivated by an effort to understand the child's ideas and if accomplished without undue attention. The clinician must strive for precision, repeating exactly what the child meant to say, rather than recoding incorrect grammatical forms into correct forms. The clinician must be careful not to cut off the child by coming in too soon before the child is completely finished. The clinician should minimize her or his own casual talking because all clinician utterances add playback time to subsequent transcription.

Two important observations that the clinician must make during sampling are discussed in a later section, Transcribing, #3, page 29). *Be sure that these transcriptional needs are attended to during each sampling session.*

---

* Note also that words such as "garage" permit either [ʒ] or [dʒ] as the final segment.

Recording

Equipment

High-quality audio recording equipment is essential for reliable phonetic transcription (Shriberg, Lotz, & Carlson, in preparation). The tape recorder, whether reel-to-reel or cassette, should be the best available to the clinician. Cassette recorders that sell for under 100 dollars generally are not adequate. Clinicians would be wise to budget for a high-quality recorder that will withstand the demands of extensive use in transcription. Recorders should have a VU meter for adjusting the input level (the automatic gain control should be bypassed if possible with an external microphone), a "review" button for ease in playback repeats, a footage counter, and a good quality loudspeaker. A high-quality microphone with a reasonably long cord should be purchased: lavalier (hung around the neck) microphones are useful with some children. The recording head and tape guides should be cleaned (according to manufacturer's instructions) after approximately every five hours of recording time, depending on temperature and humidity conditions and the type of recording tape used.

Only high-quality, low-noise tapes should be used. In our experience, discount-type brands are inadequate for phonetic transcription. Use of a 15-minute tape versus a 30-minute tape depends on whether one sample or several samples (of the same or different children) will be stored on the tape. Also, younger, less verbal children, will require a longer sampling session.

To ensure the validity, reliability, and efficiency of NPA, the importance of proper use and maintenance of high-quality audio equipment can not be over emphasized.

Procedures

Clinicians should consider carefully the acoustic characteristics of potential recording rooms. Is the room quiet? Are there any sources of noise (electrical hum, air conditioners, intermittent traffic, and so forth) that will reduce intelligibility or make transcription from a recording in any way less reliable or less efficient?

Placement of the recorder and microphone and seating arrangements also warrant proper consideration. *The microphone should be positioned on a different surface than the recorder, and maximally distant from the recorder and any other noise source.* This one technical need is, in our observation, the one most often overlooked by clinicians. The child should be positioned directly in line with the microphone with a lip-to-microphone distance of 6 to 12 inches, depending on how loud the child talks and the expected activity level of the child. Careful pretesting of the intensity setting of the child's and clinician's speech before taping the sample will ensure usable tape recordings. Ask the child to repeat some words or to count—then repeat what the child says while discretely adjusting the volume control (some children become inhibited by too much fussing with the tape recorder). The volume control should be adjusted so that the child's vowels cause the meter needle to peak just below the "distortion" area on the VU meter, while the stops and fricatives (which are less intense than vowels) remain clearly audible. Be sure that the clinician's speech also will be easily audible on playback. The recording volume control usually will be set at one-third to two-thirds of full scale. This should produce good signal-to-noise ratios at comfortable listening levels on tape playback.

Verbally identify the child and the date at both the beginning and the ending of the tape. As the taping progresses, listen for any noises that may interfere with transcription. Have the child repeat key utterances that may have been masked by transient noises, including those made by the child touching the microphone or its cord, kicking the table, dropping toys, and so forth. For the purposes of later analyses, responses to such requests will be apparent in the transcript and may be isolated from the spontaneous, continuous speech data if necessary. Again, careful attention to the acoustic quality of the tapes as the session progresses will enhance the efficiency of transcription and the reliability of the subsequent natural process analysis.

Transcribing

Data from a completed Transcription Sheet provide information on the context of each sound change. For example, knowing whether the word following a word-final consonant deletion begins with a consonant or a vowel could be useful descriptive information for later analyses. Furthermore, preservation of the entire utterance is required for most language analyses. It is possible, however, to bypass Transcription Sheets and to code process occurrence directly from live or audio taped speech. Whether or not Transcription Sheets are used, most of the procedural instructions discussed in this section will need to be considered.

Transcription Sheet

We have used a Transcription Sheet (see next page) for a live transcription and for transcription from audio recordings. Somewhat similar forms, with space provided for the interlocutor's utterances, are used by clinicians for transcribing language samples. A form that allows for analyses of all language levels, including phonology, could easily be designed. Essentially, the Transcription Sheet provides space for a *Gloss* (what the child meant to say or attempted to say) and a *Transcription* (what the child did say) for each utterance. Depending on the child's average length of utterance, two to four Transcription Sheets generally are sufficient for each 200- to 250-word sample.

In addition to the basic child identification information at the top of the sheet, we have found it important also to note the type of stimulus conditions and to comment on the child's general health and attitude at the time of the sample. For example: Does the child have a cold or active allergies? Was the child reluctant to talk?

In all stages of these procedures, it has proven prudent to use pencil (dark enough for photocopy) rather than pen!

Live Transcription versus Transcription from a Recording

As discussed, the clinician may decide to transcribe during the speech sampling rather than later from an audio recording. The advantages of transcribing the sample live (on-line) are: (1) the clinician hears the original speech signal, rather than one that has been electronically processed, (2) the clinician has available certain visual information

NPA TRANSCRIPTION SHEET

Shriberg and Kwiatkowski

John Wiley & Sons   Copyright 1980 NPA

Child _____ DOB _____
Sampling _____ Age _____
Date _____ Analysis ____
Clinician _____ Date _____

Comments on _____
Sample _____
Conditions _____

Page No. _____

Item No.	GLOSS	TRANSCRIPTION	Item No.	GLOSS	TRANSCRIPTION

on articulatory movements that may aid in transcription judgments (for example, unreleased final stops versus deleted final stops), and (3) the clinician does not have to set aside time for transcription from a tape recording.

Disadvantages to on-line transcription are: (1) the clinician must accomplish transcription while performing the necessary verbal/social interactions with the child, (2) the clinician has only one chance to transcribe an utterance—utterances that can not be transcribed must be discarded, (3) the clinician must set aside proportionally more time for Sampling because of the time needed for transcription of a sufficient number of words, and (4) the clinician will not have available a reference recording for subsequent analyses, reliability assessment, or progress monitoring. For some clinical situations, particularly with children who produce only short utterances, on-line transcription may be the method of choice. It is particularly important for future reference to annotate on-line transcriptions with information about sampling conditions and child behaviors. Ultimately, as a clinician becomes proficient in transcription, a combination of on-line transcription and transcription from a recording may provide the most reliable data.

Transcription Procedures and Conventions

For the most complete data set, the clinician should gloss and transcribe the entire speech sample. Alternatively, only a fixed number of tokens of each word might be glossed and transcribed. Because the coding procedure that follow use *only the first occurrence of each word* (see page 13 for rationale), it may be inefficient to transcribe the entire sample for some purposes—for example, for monitoring a child's progress on certain processes. For most purposes, however, it is useful to have a transcription of the entire sample. The following definitions and suggestions assume that the clinician is attempting to gloss and transcribe the entire sample.

Glossing

1. An *utterance* is defined as one or a string of spoken syllables bounded by pauses. Each utterance is entered sequentially in one of the 20 spaces (boxes) on a Transcription Sheet. Or for very brief utterances, enter two or more utterances in a box.

2. Unless constraints are required for particular language analyses, all utterances that can be glossed are included in the transcription, including all asides, false starts, repetitions, answers to wh-questions, and so forth.

3. Enter exactly what you believe the child intended to say. If the child said, for example, [hɪm doʊd], enter "him goed" in the gloss box rather than the correct, "He went." Adherance to this convention is essential for differentiating among several possible sources of phonological simplification. As described later, the transcript preserves data for a variety of linguistic analyses, but the primary goal of these procedures is to yield a valid summary of phonological process usage.

4. If a bound morpheme in an obligatory context is not represented in the transcription, place parentheses around it in the gloss. For example: "wear my boot(s) to go out" [weɪr maɪ but tə do aʊt]. Later in Coding, this word "boot(s)" will be treated as a CVCC, but the gloss will preserve the fact that the plural morpheme was assumed. Notice that this convention does not contradict (2) above; it applies *only* when a bound morpheme is not present in the transcription (compared to, for example, "him goed").

5. Gloss all casual speech forms the way a child would normally say them in conversational speech. For example: "n" (and); "m" (them); "ya" (yes); "cause" (because).

6. If all or any part of an utterance is unintelligible, enter "XXX" in the gloss box, with each X representing an unintelligible syllable. For example: "XX X go byebye."

7. If undecided between two words the child is attempting to say, write the more likely word first, separated by a slash from the second. For example: "this/it," "was/why," "the/a."

8.   Circle any utterance or portion of an utterance that you are unsure of. For example: "She's in ⟨bed⟩—get up."

9.   Gloss catenatives as they occur in casual or fast speech. For example: "gonna" (going to), "hafta" (have to), "wanna" (want to), "whatcha" (what are you), "lemme" (let me).

10.   Differentiate noun compounds (blackboard) from noun phrases (black board). The former will be treated later as a two syllable word: the latter as two words. Ritualized reduplications (for example, "bye bye") are counted as one word. Proper names (Mickey Mouse) are treated as one word only for a young child or a child with limited language.

Transcribing

1.   Phonetically transcribe all glossed utterances. Close transcription of all subphonemic behaviors such as aspiration, duration, nasalization, stop-release features, and tongue place/constriction changes is extremely useful. For the purposes of Coding (to be discussed), however, the instructions for phonetic transcription provided here will be sufficient.

2.   Although the attempt should be made to transcribe every glossed utterance, try to allow no more than three tape playbacks for each word. Generally, clinicians transcribe the "easy" segments in each word first, returning to transcribe the more difficult segments on the second and third replay. Circle any portion of the transcription about which you are particularly unsure. Although the attempt should be made to transcribe every glossed utterance, it is not efficient to persist after three playbacks; furthermore the transcription resulting from repeated playbacks may be unreliable. Utterances or portions of utterances that can not be transcribed in three playbacks, should be indicated by placing a question mark inside of a circle. If later these utterances are deemed important to the analyses, they can be attempted again.

3.   Two aspects of articulatory behavior should be visually observed during the sampling sessions. Both are difficult to transcribe from even a high-quality audio tape recording. First, characteristics of the closure of final stops /p, b/ and the alveolars /t, d/ should be observed closely. Try to determine whether the lips or tongue reached the appropriate position for these sounds in word-final position (closure for /k/ and /g/ is generally not possible to observe). Unreleased stops, in particular, usually are not audible on tape. Second, because the fricatives /f/, /v/, /θ/, and /ð/ are low-intensity sounds, they are difficult to discriminate on tape recordings. During the sampling, try to note whether the lip and tongue gestures are correct for these sounds or whether the child substitutes one for another. These notes made on-line should be used to resolve all subsequent transcription questions.

4.   Do not be concerned about the difficulty in transcribing voicing features. For the reasons discussed earlier (see p. 11), it is sometimes difficult to determine whether a sound was partially voiced or partially devoiced. Hence, sound changes involving voicing, whether a cognate substitution (e.g., [s/z] or partial voicing/devoicing, are not coded as natural processes although they are annotated in the Notes section of the Summary Sheet.

5.   Do not be concerned about the difficulty in transcribing vowels. For Unstressed Syllable Deletion, it is important to determine if any vowel was preserved. But it is not efficient to spend a lot of time considering alternative transcriptions for vowel coloring because no other process is associated with vowels. As suggested later, fine-grained analyses of processes could involve close vowel transcription (for example, whether vowels are differentially lengthened before deleted final obstruents), provided the clinician has close transcription skills.

6. Symbolization of "r" sounds is one of the most controversial areas in phonetics. It is important to observe closely the conventions listed here.

a. Use [r] for both prevocalic /r/, as in [rid] "read," and for postvocalic /r/, as in [dir] "deer."

b. Use [ɝ] for the stressed vowel, as in [bɝd] "bird."

c. Use [ɚ] for an unstressed vowel, as in [sɪstɚ] "sister."

Stressed vowel [ɝ] and unstressed vowel [ɚ] may enter into coding decisions for only Unstressed Syllable Deletion; the remaining processes in this procedure are concerned only with consonant sounds.*

Error symbolization for the prevocalic /r/ and postvocalic /r/ may take one of four forms.

a. *Deletion,* wherein "rabbit" is symbolized as [æbɪt].

b. *Substitution* of [w] in provocalic position only, wherein "rabbit" is symbolized as [wæbɪt].

c. *Partial loss of "r" coloring* (derhotacization) symbolized as [ɹ], wherein "rabbit" becomes [ɹæbɪt] and "park" becomes [pɑɹk].

d. *Substitution* of a non "r"-colored vowel in postvocalic position only, wherein "fire" becomes [fɑɪə], "park" becomes [pɑək] (note that vowel substitutions usually involve a neutralized [ə] with or without lip rounding).

As will be apparent later in the section on Coding, these arbitrary symbolization conventions must be used consistently.

7. Transcription of /l/ is often difficult, especially in postvocalic final position as in "fail" and "wheel." Before back vowels and after all vowels, /l/ is produced as a "dark" /l/, that is, as a velarized /l/, [ɫ]. In the postvocalic position, especially word final—velarized [ɫ] sounds very much like the high back vowels [ʊ] or [o]. Clinicians should try to determine if a child's postvocalic or final cluster /l/ is just normally velarized [teɪɫ], deleted (Final Consonant Deletion) [teɪ], or replaced by a high back vowel [teɪo]. We have not found it efficient to spend a lot of time pondering such decisions.

8. Transcription of glottal stops is another problematic area. As demonstrated later (Case Study #3) glottal stops do occur in many children and they are of interest in the assessment process. Clinicians should try to transcribe them if quite certain that they occur. However, although glottalization may be a natural process, reliability problems in transcribing glottal stops preclude use of this process in the formal analysis.

9. Distinctions between [w] and [ʍ] and between final [ŋ] versus [n] are not transcribed closely because they are difficult to discriminate, are of no clinical significance, and do not play a role in process coding.

---

* Partial loss of "r"-coloring on [ɝ] is symbolized as [ɝ̮]; partial loss of "r"-coloring on [ɚ] is symbolized as [ɚ̮]. All symbolization used in NPA follows a system developed expressly to meet clinical needs (Shriberg & Kent, in preparation)

Preparation for Notes and Additional Analyses

As you listen to the audio tape or live sample and transcribe each utterance, it is efficient to begin making notes about other aspects of the child's speech. Once familiar with the NPA procedure, it will be easy to identify which factors in a child's speech production are process related and which are not. Included among those that are not are such behaviors as: additions, distortions, vowel errors, nonprocess substitutions, speaking rate and rhythm, voice quality, and so forth. Part III, Guidelines for Additional Analyses, suggests a variety of factors which can be reviewed as you transcribe your sample. Making notes on these factors as they occur while you are transcribing provides an efficient headstart on completing the additional analyses.

Review and Discussion Questions (See Appendix B for Answers)

1. Describe some ways to obtain a continuous speech sample from a child. How can you ensure that the child will say some otherwise infrequently occurring sounds (23)?
2. What two functions do clinicians' verbalizations serve during sampling (24)?
3. Describe in sequence how you would set up the room and your recording equipment to obtain a speech sample from a child. What factors will optimize the quality of the recording (25)?
4. While obtaining a continuous speech sample from a child, what two classes of articulatory behaviors should you observe closely as the child talks (29)?
5. What is meant by the following entries on the Transcription Sheet?
    a. two cat(s)
    b. see the/a man
    c. he get his brush
    d. walk
6. How would you enter each of the following child utterances in the gloss box?
    a. He be happy
    b. eat em
    c. I hafta go
    d. snowsuit

7. Transcribe the following words, using the appropriate symbolization conventions for /r/, /ɜ˞/, and /ɚ/.

   a. fire

   b. fur

   c. brother

8. Transcribe the following words, as they would be said by a child who has a *partial* loss of r-coloring (derhotacization).

   a. Kurt

   b. mother

   c. dark

   d. red

9. Transcribe the following words as they might be said by a child who has a *complete* loss of r-coloring, that is, vowel substitution.

   a. Kurt

   b. mother

   c. dark

Coding

Coding procedures are divided into two operations: (1) entering selected words from the Transcription Sheet into appropriate boxes on the Coding Sheets, and (2) assigning a code to each consonant, consonant cluster, and polysyllabic word entered on the Coding Sheets (see Sample NPA Analysis). Until completely familiar with coding operations, the clinician should follow this two-stage process—enter all words first, then return to each word for coding. The clinician will later be able to save time by coding each word immediately as it is entered on a Coding Sheet.

Procedures for Entering Words on the Coding Sheets

1. Three Coding Sheets (see pages 34–36) each provide columns in which to enter words taken from the Transcription Sheets. Seven columns are provided for entering monosyllabic words of five basic canonical shapes, and for entering two-syllable and three-plus-syllable words. The sheets are divided so as to group words of similar target consonants. Sheet A is for nasals, glides, and liquids; Sheet B is for stops; and Sheet C is for fricatives and affricates. Spaces for sounds that do not occur in that position (for example, initial [ŋ], final [w] are screened out on the Coding Sheets.)

2. The underlined consonant in Column 1 (C̲V), Column 2 (V̲C), and Column 3 (CV̲C)

is the target consonant for each word in the gloss. It is this target sound that determines where each gloss and transcription should be entered on the Coding Sheets. If the child attempts to say the word "pig," for example, both the gloss and the transcription are entered on Sheet B, Column 3, in the row for /g/, that is, CV$\underline{C}$. Importantly, for the purpose of entering words it does not matter whether or not a child says a word correctly, or whether he or she says it incorrectly. For example, the word "pig" might be said as [pɪ], or [bid], or [pɪdə]. Because the word attempted, "pig," is a CVC and because it ends in "g," data are *always* entered in the CV$\underline{C}$ column (Column 3) and "g" row for this word.

3. Column 4 on each of the Coding Sheets is for words that contain clusters in the initial position; Column 5 on each sheet is for words that have final clusters. To save space, words in the gloss which have several types of canonical forms are entered in each column, provided that the word has an initial cluster (Column 4) or a final cluster (Column 5). The symbol "Cⁿ" in each column indicates that the cluster, as it would be represented phonetically in the gloss, may have two or more members. For example, the word "glimpsed" actually ends in a cluster containing four segments, [mpst]. The word "glimpsed" would be entered together with a transcription of the child's attempt at this word on Sheet B, Column 5 (for final consonant clusters) in the row for /t/, that is, (C)VCⁿ. Similarly, if a child said [pun] for "spoon" both words would be entered in the appropriate boxes on Coding Sheet C, Column 4 (for initial clusters), in the row for /s/, that is, $\underline{C}$nⁿV(C). *Words that both begin and end with clusters are arbitrarily entered in Column 5, in the row for the final consonant in the cluster.* For example, the word "plants" [plænts], CCVCC$\underline{C}$, is entered on Sheet C, Column 5, in the row for /s/; the word "stamped" [stæmpt], CCVCC$\underline{C}$ is entered on Sheet B, Column 5, in the row for /t/.

4. Two-syllable words and words of three or more syllables are entered in Columns 6 and 7, respectively. The *first consonant in the word determines the row entry.* For example, "walking" is entered on Sheet A, Column 6, in the row for /w/; "elephant" is entered on Sheet A, Column 7, in the row for /l/.

5. When entering words on the coding sheet, enter the Item Number from which the word was obtained in the upper left-hand corner of the gloss box (e.g., $\boxed{^{22}\text{cat}}$). Identifying the utterance (item) from which the word was taken facilitates reviewing the Coding and Transcription Sheets while completing additional analyses (to be discussed later in the text).

6. Use Kenyon and Knott's phonetic dictionary (Kenyon, J. S., & Knott, T. A. *A Pronouncing Dictionary of American English,* Springfield, Massachusetts: G. & C. Merriam Company, 1953) as the reference for all canonical forms. Optional final syllabics (for example, "fountain" [fɑʊntn̩], CVCCC, versus [fɑʊntən], CVCCVC, are not critical to observe for the coding rules to follow.

7. Do not enter words on the Coding Sheet which ordinarily are reduced in casual or fast speech and appear as such in the Gloss; (for example, "and" [n̩], "them [m̩]. The general idea is to avoid coding a word that indicates the presence of a process when the word normally would be said that way in casual or fast speech (recall in the text that natural processes are attested in just this way). Whenever in doubt about such qualifications, particularly when a word occurs in an unstressed position in the string, do not enter the word on the Coding Sheet.

8. Do not enter words on the Coding Sheet which have been circled as questionable on the Transcription Sheet. Words with parentheses around bound morphemes, however, may be entered in the appropriate column. For example, "boot(s)" said as [but] would be entered in Column 5 (see Glossing, #4, page 28, for this example).

9. As discussed in the text, a 200- to 250-word sample will normally include approximately 80 to 100 different words on the Transcription Sheet. To keep track of words

NPA CODING SHEET

Shriberg and Kwiatkowski
John Wiley & Sons   Copyright 1980 NPA

Child _____   DOB _____
Sampling _____   Age _____
Date _____   Analysis _____
Clinician _____   Date _____

Coding Sheet: [A] Nasals; Glides; Liquids
Page No. _____

Total Words Entered _____
Sounds: [m, n, ŋ, w, j, l, r]

Sound	**1** CV Gloss	Trans.	Code	**2** VC Gloss	Trans.	Code	**3** CVC Gloss	Trans.	Code	**4** C^n V(C) Gloss	Trans.	Code	**5** (C)VC^n Gloss	Trans.	Code	**6** Two-Syllable Gloss	Trans.	Code	**7** Three⁺ Syllable Gloss	Trans.	Code
m																					
n																					
ŋ																					
w																					
j																					
l																					
r																					

NPA CODING SHEET

Shriberg and Kwiatkowski
John Wiley, & Sons   Copyright 1980 NPA

Child _____   DOB _____
Sampling _____ Analysis _____   Age _____
Date _____   Date _____
Clinician _____

Coding Sheet: [B] Stops
Page No. _____

Total Words Entered _____
Sounds: [p, b, t, d, k, g.]

Sound	1 CV			2 VC			3 CVC			4 C^n V(C)			5 (C) VC^n			6 Two-Syllable			7 Three⁺ Syllable		
	Gloss	Trans.	Code	Gloss	Trans.	Code	Gloss	Trans.	Code	Gloss	Trans.	Code	Gloss	Trans.	Code	Gloss	Trans.	Code	Gloss	Trans.	Code
p																					
b																					
t																					
d																					
k																					
g																					

NPA CODING SHEET

Shriberg and Kwiatkowski   Copyright 1980 NPA
John Wiley & Sons

Child _____   DOB _____
Sampling _____   Age _____
Date _____   Analysis _____
Date _____
Clinician _____

Coding Sheet: [C] Fricatives; Affricates
Page No. _____

Total Words Entered _____
Sounds: [h, f, v, θ, ð, s, z, ʃ, ʒ, tʃ, dʒ]

Sound	**1** CV			**2** VC			**3** CVC			**4** Cⁿ V(C)				**5** (C) VCⁿ				**6** Two-Syllable				**7** Three⁺ Syllable		
	Gloss	Trans.	Code	Gloss	Trans.	Code	Gloss	Trans.	Code	Gloss	Trans.	Code		Gloss	Trans.	Code		Gloss	Trans.	Code		Gloss	Trans.	Code
h																								
f																								
v																								
θ																								
ð																								
s																								
z																								
ʃ																								
ʒ																								
tʃ																								
dʒ																								

entered on the Coding Sheet it is helpful to place a small check just above each word (see sample). A checked word will usually be the first occurrence of that word in the transcription.

10. If not all sounds have been sampled (e.g., /ʃ/, /dʒ/) after 80 to 100 words have been entered for Coding, it is inefficient to continue entering words as they occur sequentially in the transcript. Rather, just look ahead in the transcript for sounds that are missing; enter utterances containing those words as necessary until all sounds have been sampled.

11. The spaces allotted on the three Coding Sheets should be sufficient for a 250-word sample. More room might be needed for older children or for children who say more polysyllabic words. Use additional sheets as required.

Procedures for Coding Words

As discussed earlier in this text (pages 11–12), we take position that some natural processes are more likely than others to underlie a given sound change. The sequence of Coding procedures to be described in this section accounts for these assumptions. *It is essential, therefore, to proceed through the Coding process exactly in the order described next. Failure to follow this sequence yields incorrect data for all subsequent analyses.*

1. Coding of Correct Consonants and Correct Consonant Clusters—"C"

The Coding process begins with inspection of all words entered on the three Coding Sheets (A, B, C) to determine which consonants and consonant clusters in Columns 1 through 5 (monosyllabic words only) were said correctly by the child. If the child said the consonant or consonant cluster correctly, enter "C" in the appropriate box on the Coding Sheet, otherwise, leave the box blank.

The following instructions concerning distortions, additions, and voicing errors are important to observe, both in deciding whether a target sound is correct and later, in coding each process.

a. Phonetic *distortions* of sounds, such as *dentalization, lateralization,* and *deaspiration* do not disqualify a sound from being correct ("C"). For example, [s̺] is coded as "C." Phonetic distortions also do not disqualify a sound change resulting from a process. For example, [s/ʃ] and [s̺/ʃ] are both coded as Palatal Fronting (to be described). The fact that the sound that replaced the target sound was itself distorted [s̺/ʃ] does not obviate Palatal Fronting as the explanatory process.

b. *Additions* are treated exactly the same way as distortions. If "cars" is said as [kɑrks], the final cluster is still considered correct and coded as "C." Addition errors are infrequent. Generally, they are restricted to only particular lexical items or occur during a stage of acquisition or management when new and old responses are equiprobable, for example, [pfʌn] or [fpʌn] for "fun," [tsænd] or [stænd] for "sand."

c. Voicing errors also do not disqualify a sound from being considered correct, "C." For example, "zoo" said as [su] is coded as "C."*

Distortions, additions, and voicing errors are considered phonetic-level errors. These errors can be described in the Notes section at the bottom of the Summary Sheet,

---

* Some clinicians who have used the NPA procedure have taken to using "Ȼ" (pronounced "see-bar") to indicate a sound that is "correct" only by the definitions given here. Hence "C" is used for sounds fully correct—"Ȼ" is used to remind clinicians that the sound in question (or sounds, in the case of Unstressed Syllable Deletion) are not "really" correct.

and they become part of the additional analyses procedures (Phonetic Analysis) described later. The point here is that for reliable NPA coding, all "errors" of this type must be treated as described above.

One more reminder about "r" sounds. Recall that natural process coding is concerned only with the consonant /r/, not the vowels, /ɝ/ or /ɚ/)except as these two vowel sounds may be involved in syllable deletion in polysyllabic words). A derhotacized /r/, [ṟ], as with other distortions, is considered "C." Other error types for /r/, such as [w/r], [ə/r] (as in [faɪə] for "fire"), and /r/ deletions; are considered errors and are coded according to the procedures that follow.

2. Coding of Initial Consonant Deletions—"ø"

Initial consonant deletion is not considered to be a natural process, but it is useful to code occurrences of initial consonant deletions on the NPA Coding Sheets. If the initial consonant is deleted in any word in Columns 1, 3, or 5, enter "ø" in the appropriate box. Words that should begin with consonant clusters are excluded from this coding; enter "ø" *only* when a child has deleted an initial singleton consonant target.

3. Coding of the Eight Natural Processes

To this point in the coding process, some boxes on the Coding Sheets will contain "C" (and/or "₵") and some boxes for initial consonants will contain "ø." To complete the Coding procedures, each of the eight processes is coded *in the sequence presented next.* For the first process that follows, for example, go through each Coding Sheet to see which final consonant targets should be coded as FCD. Be sure to take each process one at a time, going through all appropriate words on each Coding Sheet (A, B, C) to determine whether the process code should be entered in the box. When thoroughly familiar with all Coding procedures it is possible for a clinician to take "short cuts" that save time without loss of accuracy. Coding instructions begin on page 39.

Explanations for Coding Examples (pages 39 to 42)

Try first to learn the referent for each column number as given on pages 32—33. For example, Column 1 is for words that have a CV morpheme structure as their target. Remember that words are entered on Coding Sheets by the target sound as given in the Gloss *not* by what the child actually said.

(1)	[kw→gw] = "C"	Voicing errors do not disqualify a sound from being correct.
(2)	[s→ṣ] = "C"	Distortions do not disqualify a sound from being correct.
(3)	[tʃ→ʃ] = Uncoded	To be coded as Stopping a fricative or affricate must be replaced by a phonemic stop; otherwise leave blank.
(4)	—	Both boxes are left uncoded *at this point* in the Coding sequence. For consonants in Columns 4 and 5 to be considered for Stopping (or for Velar Fronting, Palatal Fronting, and Liquid Simplification) the consonant cluster in the word must be coded "C"; otherwise leave blank.
(5)	[ʃ→s] = PF	Lateralization of the /s/, [s] does not disqualify coding as Palatal Fronting.

Process	Code	Procedure	Examples				Explanation [a]

			Column Number	Gloss	Transcription	Code	
1. Final Consonant Deletion	FCD	Enter FCD in the Code column only if the final consonant is *deleted*; otherwise leave blank. If *any* phonemic consonant is present in the final position, do *not* score as FCD. NOTE: Although a glottal stop [ʔ] is *not* a phoneme of American English, reliability problems in transcribing glottal stops are marked. Hence, when a glottal stop *is* entered for a final (or an initial consonant) the relevant box is simply left blank; that is, the box is left uncodable.	2	on	ɔ	FCD	
			2	in	ɪn	C	
			3	Tim	dɪ	C ¦ FCD	
			3	quack	gwæ	C ¦ FCD	
			4	snap	snæʔ	C	(1)

			Column Number	Gloss	Transcription	Code	
2. Velar Fronting	VF	Inspect all CV, VC, and CVC target words that contain uncoded /k/ or /g/. Include also words in Columns 4 and 5 if the cluster was said correctly. Enter VF in the appropriate box if /k/ or /g/ is *replaced by* [t] or [d]; otherwise leave blank.	3	good	dʊd	VF ¦ C	
			3	get	tɛ	VF ¦ FCD	
			3	Mack	mæt	C ¦ VF	
			4	trick	trɪt	C ¦ VF	

[a] For explanation of numbered EXAMPLES, see pages 38 and 43.

Process	Code	Procedure	Column Number	Gloss	Transcription	Code	Explanation [a]
3. Stopping	S	Inspect all CV, VC, and CVC target words that contain uncoded /θ/, /ð/, /f/, /v/, /s/, /z/, /ʃ/, /ʒ/, /tʃ/, and /dʒ/. Include also words with these sounds in Columns 4 and 5 if the cluster was said correctly.	1	so	ʂoʊ	C	(2)
			2	off	ɔp	S	
		Enter S in the appropriate box if any of these sounds has been *replaced by* any phonemic stop; otherwise, leave blank. Replacement by a glottal stop does *not* meet this response definition; replacement must be by one of the six phonemic stops.	3	catch	kæʃ	C	(3)
			3	gym	dɪm	s c	
			3	he's	hid	c s	
			3	face	beɪt	s s	(4)
			5	jump	dʌm	s s	
			6	sink	ʔɪŋk	c	
4. Palatal Fronting	PF	Inspect all CV, VC, and CVC target words that contain /ʃ/, /ʒ/, /tʃ/, or /dʒ/. Include also words in Columns 4 and 5 if the cluster was said correctly.	1	shoe	ðu	PF	(5)
			1	she	si	PF	
			1	choo	tu	S	
		Enter PF if any of these four sounds has been *replaced by* any phoneme *more* anterior (alveolar, lingua-dental, bilabial); otherwise, leave blank.	3	chair	heir	c	(6)
			3	fish	pɪs	s c	
			5	shirt	tʃɜtʃ		

a For explanation of numbered EXAMPLES, see pages 38 and 43.

Process	Code	Procedure	Examples				Explanation [a]
			Column Number	Gloss	Transcription	Code	
5. Liquid Simplification	LS	Inspect all CV, VC, and CVC target words that contain uncoded consonant /l/ or /r/ (recall that vowels /ɜ/ and /ɚ/ are excluded from this analysis). Include also words in Columns 4 and 5 if the cluster was said correctly. Enter LS if either of these two sounds is *replaced by a vowel* or [w] or [j] otherwise, leave blank.	1	lay	peɪ		(7)
			2	all	ɔ	FCD	(8)
			3	right	waɪ	LS ¦ FCD	
			3	wait	leɪt	C	(9)
6. Assimilation Progressive and Regressive	PA RA	Inspect all uncoded consonants in CVC words. Do *not* inspect words in Columns 4 and 5. Enter PA or RA if the final or initial consonant, respectively has been *replaced by a phoneme that resembles it* (i.e., similar place, manner, voicing features) or is the same as the other consonant—even if the other consonant has been deleted. Processes may be ordered such that assimilation operates before the "culprit" is deleted, as in the last two examples here (see also page 12 and the description of Assimilation in Summarizing).	3	gate	geɪk	C ¦ PA	
			3	cut	kʌk	C ¦ PA	
			3	pin	nɪ	RA ¦ FCD	
			3	cup	ʌk	ø ¦ PA	

[a] For explanation of numbered EXAMPLES, see page 43.

Process	Code	Procedure
7. Cluster Reduction	CR	Inspect all uncoded clusters (clusters not coded "C") in Columns 4 and 5. Enter CR if one or more members of the cluster is *deleted or replaced by another phoneme*; otherwise, enter "C."
8. Unstressed Syllable Deletion	USD	Inspect all words in Columns 6 and 7. Enter USD if any syllable has been en-tirely *deleted*. Deletion requires that no part of the syllable or any substitution for it remain; otherwise enter "C." Technically, only unstressed syllables should be inspected. Owing to the dif-ficulty in determining which syllable is retained, however, deletion of any syl-lable in the word qualifies as USD.

Examples

Explanation [a]

Column Number	Gloss	Transcription	Code	
4	smile	maɪ	CR	(10)
4	jump	dʒʌp	C CR	
4	clothes	ko	CR	(11)
5	drink	drɪɡ	C CR	
5	first	hir	CR	

Column Number	Gloss	Transcription	Code	
6	empty	ɛmpɪ	C	(12)
6	different	dɪpə	C	
6	except	tɛpt	USD	
7	another	na	USD	

[a] For explanation of numbered EXAMPLES, see page 43.

(6) [tʃ→h] = Uncoded

Palatal Fronting requires a sound change from a palatal to a sound *more anterior;* otherwise leave blank.

(7) [l→p] = Uncoded

This sound change is not included among those that qualify as Liquid Simplification.

(8) [l→ø] = FCD

The final /l/ deletion would already have been coded as Final Consonant Deletion. This example illustrates the need to proceed through the eight processes in the order given.

(9) [w→l] = Uncoded

This example is a foil. Liquid Simplification includes sound changes *only* for target /l/ and target /r/.

(10) [sm→m] = CR
[l→ø] = Uncoded

Although final /l/ is deleted, the box is left uncoded because the initial cluster is not coded "C" (see instructions for Final Consonant Deletion).

(11) [kl→l] = CR
[z→ø] = Uncoded

As in (10) above, the final deletion is not coded because the initial cluster is not coded "C." Note the importance of knowing the correct canonical structure of words: "clothes" [kloz] is a CVC, *not* a CVCC [kloðz].

(12) —

This example illustrates the importance of entering words on the Coding Sheets according to their usual, reduced form in casual speech. Although "different" is a three-syllable word, it commonly is said as a two-syllable word [dɪfrɛnt]; therefore, it is properly entered in Column 6, not Column 7.

If these procedures are followed carefully, some words will be fully or in part, uncoded (blank boxes). Uncoded segments on the Coding Sheets remain available for the purposes of the Summary Sheet analyses and later, for additional close analyses. For example, because words containing clusters are not used for decisions about Velar Fronting, Stopping, Palatal Fronting, or Liquid Simplification, a word such as "just" said as [dʌt], will be coded only for Cluster Reduction (the left box for the initial consonant will be left blank). The reasoning here is to avoid coding the [d/dʒ] as Stopping, when other process explanations (phonological derivations) could be proposed; for example, Cluster Reduction of the final cluster /st/, followed by Regressive Assimilation reducing the initial affricate /dʒ/ to the stop [d]. For the Summary Sheet section of Phonetic Inventory, however (to be discussed next), all glossed examples of a sound are inspected. The word "just," for example, may be the only instance in the gloss of [dʒ] and it would be considered as "glossed, but not correct" (to be described).

It is useful to restate here that not all sound changes which occur in a sample are "accounted for" by natural processes. In the Guidelines for Interpretation and Additional Analyses that follow, division of all sound changes into one of five sources will be explained in detail.

Review and Discussion Questions (See Appendix B for Answers)

1. Which words on a Transcription Sheet are entered on Coding sheets? Which words are not?

2. For each of the following words, list its appropriate place of entry on the Coding Sheet (A, B, or C), Column (1–7), and Row (each of the phonemes). For example, a child's attempt to say the word "dogs," no matter how it was actually articulated, will *always* be entered on Sheet C, Column 5, Row /z/.

   a. go

   b. goes

   c. walk

   d. walked

   e. walking

   f. stew

   g. Brad's

   h. her

   i. pepper

3. What would you do if you were unsure of the proper canonical form of a word in the gloss?

4. How well can you code words? Have you actually tried yet? Using Transcription Sheets from any of the sample NPA's in this text—and blank Coding Sheets—try coding several dozen words. Is your interjudge agreement 100%? 95%? Less? Review the appropriate readings and keep coding words until you are completely familiar and competent with the procedures for Coding as described on pages 32 to 43. It is easy—once you get the hang of it!

Summarizing

A completed Summary Sheet (see page 46) provides the clinician with a one-page description of a child's speech. Summary Sheet data provide the "purest" view of the child's use of the eight natural processes in the sense that all questionable glosses and questionable transcriptions have been removed in the previous Coding procedures.

Furthermore, the process Coding procedures have been designed to be conservative—to achieve the reliability needed for clinical practice and clinical research. Fine-grained analyses of *all* sound changes in the transcriptions (including uncoded sound changes) are explained in the Guidelines to Interpretation and Additional Analyses; here we describe procedures for deriving the three areas of information on the one-page Summary Sheet: (1) The Phonetic Inventory, (2) The Eight Natural Processes, and (3) Notes.

The Phonetic Inventory

The first four rows on the Summary Sheet provide a summary of the child's use of the 24 consonants in continuous speech. While not process data itself, this information is needed to interpret the process data that follow. As indicated by the four headings below, this summary asks whether or not each sound is in the child's inventory (the phonetic repertoire). Whether or not a child always uses a sound in the right place is another matter (in part, the phonological system).

Each of the 24 consonants is given an "X" in ONLY ONE of the four rows, depending on its status as determined from the *Coding Sheets only*. **All words on all Coding Sheets are inspected, including two-syllable and three-plus syllable words.** Proceed sound by sound to determine which of these four categories should be marked with an "X."

CORRECT ANYWHERE

Place an "X" in this row if a sound is articulated correctly in *any* word. Even if a sound is correct in only one word, it qualifies as CORRECT ANYWHERE. As before, distortions, additions, and voicing errors do not disqualify a sound from being correct.

OR

APPEARS ANYWHERE

Place an "X" in this row if a sound appears anywhere on the Coding Sheet as a substitution for another sound. Although never used correctly as the target sound (that is, the sound is not CORRECT ANYWHERE), the sound *is* demonstrably in the child's phonetic inventory when an "X" is placed in this row. Again, *even one appearance* of the sound as a substitution is sufficient for placing an "X" in APPEARS ANYWHERE.

OR

GLOSSED, BUT NEVER CORRECT AND NEVER APPEARS ANYWHERE

Place an "X" in this row if the target sound was called for in at least one glossed word, but was never said correctly and never appeared correctly as a substitution.

OR

NEVER GLOSSED; NEVER APPEARS ANYWHERE

Place an "X" in this row if the target sound was never called for in any words on the Coding Sheet and never appears as a substitution.

NPA SUMMARY SHEET

Shriberg and Kwiatkowski   Copyright 1980 NPA
John Wiley & Sons

Child _____ DOB _____
Sampling _____   Age _____
Date _____   Analysis _____
Clinician _____   Date _____

Total Words
Entered
(A + B + C)

PROCESS SYMBOLS

✓ Always Occurs
Ø Sometimes Occurs
O Never Occurs
- No Data Available

Phonetic Inventory

	m	n	ŋ	w	j	p	b	t	d	k	g	h	f	v	θ	ð	s	z	ʃ	ʒ	tʃ	dʒ	l	r
Correct Anywhere →																									
Appears Anywhere →																									
Glossed Never Correct Never Appears →																									
Never Glossed; Never Appears →																									

1 Final Consonant Deletion →

2 Velar Fronting   Initial →   Final →

3 Stopping   Initial →   Final →

4 Palatal Fronting   Initial →   Final →

5 Liquid ↕ Simplification

6 Progressive Assimilations   Regressive Assimilations

7 Cluster Reduction   Correct   Reduced
Initial Clusters →
Final Clusters →

8 Unstressed Syllable Deletion

Two Syllable		Three⁺ Syllable	
n	n	n	n
% Deletions	Deletions	Deletions	% Deletions

Notes:

These phonetic data, as well as the process data to follow, are taken entirely from the Coding Sheets. Because the words on the Coding Sheets represent only 40 percent of the data, it is tempting to check the Transcription Sheet to see if the remaining words would alter the decisions. For standardization consistency, however, we use only the words on the Coding Sheets. If the Transcription does indicate a difference that is considered important for the purpose at hand, it can be noted in the Notes section on the Summary Sheet and inspected later (to be discussed in detail in Guidelines for Interpretation and Additional Analyses).

The Eight Natural Processes

(1) *Final Consonant Deletion*
(2) *Velar Fronting*
(3) *Stopping*
(4) *Palatal Fronting*
(5) *Liquid Simplification*

ALWAYS $\checkmark$ =

SOMETIMES $\oslash$ =

NEVER $\bigcirc$ =

NO DATA — =

A child's status on each of these five processes is also *determined solely from the Coding Sheets.*

Status on each of the five processes is summarized in one of four ways.

The process is used whenever the morpheme conditions (for Coding) are met; that is, the process ALWAYS applies.

The process is used SOMETIMES when the morpheme structure conditions are met.

The process is NEVER used when the morpheme structure conditions are met.

NO DATA are available; that is, the sample does not contain morpheme structure conditions to test the process. For each process, proceed through the Coding Sheets to determine which of the four symbols above to enter in the box for target consonants. Notice that these categorical decisions sometimes result from just one datum on a Coding Sheet. If coding for a particular process is based on only one or a few occurrences, this number can be written in the corner of the appropriate box (for example, "1/1"). Clinicians may wish to calculate percentages for certain process usage and enter these figures in the appropriate box.

It is important to note here that a "O" for any sound on the Summary Sheet can reflect one of two facts: (1) the process has a chance to occur and does not, or (2) the process does not occur because a process earlier in the summary sequence *always occurs.* For example, if Stopping "always occurs" ("$\checkmark$") on /f/, no other process can occur for /f/. A "√" in the column for any sound will result in a "O" for all lower boxes (i.e., all other processes that possibly could have occurred for that sound will be "O").

(6) *Assimilation*

Boxes are available to indicate whether a sound is ever the "victim" of an assimilation process and to identify the "culprit" and the "intruder." For example, if "face" is said as [feɪf] enter f→f/s in the box under Progressive Assimilation. In this example, /f/ is both the "culprit" and the "intruder" in the Progressive Assimilation process that affects the "victim," /s/. If "dog" is said [gɔg], enter g/d←g in the box under Regressive Assimilation. In this second example, /g/ is both the culprit and the intruder, and /d/ is the victim.

If "pan" is said as [mæ], enter m/p←n in the box under Regressive Assimilation. In this third example, the assumption is that two processes operated in an ordered relationship: Regressive Assimilation of the nasal feature (here the "culprit" /n/ is *not* identical to the intruder, /m/) and Final Consonant Deletion. As discussed in the text, this is the only such combination (ordered derivation) of two processes that may be coded.

(7) *Cluster Reduction*

Cluster Reduction is summarized in a straight-forward manner because of the variety of phonetic detail involved. Word-initial and word-final clusters coded in the Coding Sheets are entered in the appropriate boxes, according to whether the cluster was said correctly or reduced. Correct clusters, whether observed only once or more than once, are simply entered side by side in the appropriate box, for example: sp,, st, sk, br, bl, and so forth. Reduced clusters, whether observed only once or more than once, are entered in the appropriate box using substitution notation, for example: bw/br, k/sk, t/rt (final), and so forth.*

---

* Another convention some clinicians have adopted (recall the "Ɛ" convention, footnoted on page 37) is to underline clusters that contain a morphological marker. For example, "cats [ts]; "splashed" [spl], [ʃt]. We have used this convention in all analyses in this text; such conventions facilitate the additional analyses of morphological factors as described in Part III.

(8) *Unstressed Syllable Deletion*

Unstressed Syllable Deletion in two-syllable and three-plus-syllable words is summarized still differently from the other seven processes. In the box to the right of "**n**" enter as glossed, the total number of two-syllable (Column 6) and three-plus syllable (Column 7) words, respectively. Then enter in each respective box, the number of two-syllable and three-plus-syllable words coded as USD. Calculate the percentage of words in which an unstressed syllable was deleted and enter these figures in the remaining two boxes.

Notes

All observations that may be of clinical interest are annotated here. The amount of material in this Notes section will vary, depending on whether additional analyses are undertaken. If additional analyses along the lines described in Part III are accomplished, the Notes section might simply contain the phrase, "See additional analyses."

Review and Discussion Questions

1. Are data for the Phonetic Inventory and the Eight Natural Processes taken from the Transcription Sheets, the Coding Sheets, or from both sources?

2. Does the information on the Summary Sheet provide the clinician with an "in-depth" view of the child's phonology? Does this information allow the clinician to make a judgment about the possible cause of the developmental phonological disorder? About the predicted course of speech acquisition? About differential management needs and choice of program focus?

3. Have you actually tried Summarizing yet? Our suggestion here is precisely the same as that offered earlier for Coding. The Sample NPA Analysis to follow and the Case Studies in Part II will allow for ample practice in situations that might come up in Summarizing—indeed, these studies were selected to illustrate the variety of sound changes seen in children. Practice until you feel competent—until your interjudge agreement with the Summary Sheet data provided approaches 100 percent!

Sample NPA Analysis

This sample NPA was selected to illustrate the procedure because the child uses many of the Eight Natural Processes. For simplicity, all diacritic symbols in the original transcription have been removed or modified. The speech sample totals 235 glossed words, with 93 words coded (checked) for natural process coding.

This sample, as well as the others presented in the case studies (Part IV), also can be used to test understanding of NPA procedures. For example, by completing some blank Coding Sheets and a blank Summary Sheet—using the data presented on the Transcription Sheets—you can test your knowledge of all Coding and Summarizing procedures. Compare your Coding and Summary sheets to those presented on pages 51 to 57; then, reread the appropriate sections to resolve any differences.

Child Jack DOB _____ Age 5-10
Sampling Analysis
Date _____ Date _____
Clinician _____

Comments on Jack responded readily to all
Sample questions and prompts.
Conditions

NPA CODING SHEET

Shriberg and Kwiatkowski Copyright 1980 NPA
John Wiley & Sons

Item No.	GLOSS	TRANSCRIPTION
1	John	dɔn
2	no	no
3	I dunno	a dʌnor
4	(looks) like it(s) gonna rain	fwrf wark (it) trnə wein
5	x..(approx..15)..to rain	tu wein
6	no not too much	nor na tu m
7	my mom won't let me	mai mam worn we mi
8	uh uh	ʌʔʌ
9	I dunno	a dʌnor
10	I put on my raincoat	ai tut ɔn mai weintot

Item No.	GLOSS	TRANSCRIPTION
11	an(d) I take out my umbrella	ən ai teik ar mai (n)weda
12	mom don't let me wear my boot(s) to go out	mam dou we mi fwer ma bu ta do ar
13	I only have winter boot(s)	a orni hae wɪnə but
14	when (it's) hot an(d) sweaty	wen tʌ hat ne wedi
15	pretty soon (it's) coming up	widi (?)un dʌ hʌmɪŋ ʌp
16	x sometime xxx xx for one thing	x tʌmtaɪn xxxxx hʌ wʌn tɪŋ
17	I dunno	ʌ dʌnʊ
18	open my present (s) for one thing	ʌʊn ɪʌn uedɔ ɔ tʌ wʌn tɪŋ
19	nuh	nʌ
20	I dunno	a dono

Child Jack DOB _____
Sampling _____ Age 5-10 Analysis _____
Date _____ Date _____
Clinician _____

NPA TRANSCRIPTION SHEET
Shriberg and Kwiatkowski
John Wiley & Sons
Copyright 1980 NPA

Comments on _____
Sample _____
Conditions _____

Item No.	GLOSS	TRANSCRIPTION
21	a pair, no, a pair of rainboot(s)	ʌ pe no ʌ pe ə weɪnbut
22	a cake xxxx candle	ʌ teɪk xxxx tænʌ
23	xxxx, about this many	xxxx əbaʊ dɪt meni
24	six xxxxx big a number six	hɪk xxxxx baɪ ə nʌmə hɪk
25	xxxx number six on the candle	xxxx nʌmbə hɪk ɔ (bʌ) hænə
26	or you write the number six in	haʊ ju waɪt tʌ nʌmə hɪk? ɪn
27	I know	a noʊ
28	have a number six (go) on my cake	hæb ə nʌmbə hɪk x ɔ maɪ teɪk
29	a number six candle on my cake	ə nʌmə hɪk hæno ɔ maɪ teɪk
30	blow it	gwoʊ it
31	my dad usually take(s) picture(s) of me blowing it	maɪ dæ (wʌbdi) keɪ (kɪ)kʌ ʌ mi wodi ɪt
32	xxxxx take picture(s) while I blow it out	xxxxx peɪk (pɪkʌ) waɪ(l) aɪ woʊ ɪ aʊt
33	a matchbox car	ə mæbʌ kɔ
34	I have lot(s) of matchbox car(s)	haɪ hæb wɔt ə mæʔbə kɔ
35	all sort(s) of kinda	ɔ tɔt əb taɪn
36	I don't like to get repeats	aɪ doʊn fwaɪk tu (du fwɪpit)
37	I have one type all fill(ed) up and the other(s) are empty	aɪ hæ wʌn taɪ aʊ hi ʌp æn tʌ ʌv empi aʊ
38	they keep making different kinda	do hi meɪkɪŋ dɪpə haɪnd
39	sometime xxx repeat	hʌmpa xxx wipit
40	uh huh, went to Green Bay	ʌhʌ wɛn tu grinbeɪ

Child __Jack__   DOB _____ Age __5-10__
Sampling _____ Analysis _____
Date _____ Date _____
Clinician _____

NPA TRANSCRIPTION SHEET
Shriberg and Kwiatkowski
John Wiley & Sons   Copyright 1980 NPA

Comments on
Sample
Conditions

Item No.	GLOSS	TRANSCRIPTION
41	just stay in the hotel	dʌ? teɪ ɪn tʌ hoteʌ
→42	sometime we went to a x	hʌmpaɪm wi went (ʧ) ə tu
43	one time we went to a train station	wʌn taɪm wi went tu ə weɪn teɪntɪn
44	train station	weɪn teɪntɪn
45	uh huh	ʌha
46	we got a chance to ride on the train	wi dat ə (tænt) tu waɪ ɔn dʌ weɪn
47	I dunno	ʌ dʌno
48	a little ride	ə wɪdi waɪ
49	x have to stop two time(s)	x hæp pu dap tu taɪm
50	to open the gate	ʌp uʌdo ʌt peɪ

Item No.	GLOSS	TRANSCRIPTION
51	raise hi was the last one	tɔ hi ʌn dʌ hæ? wʌn
52	uh huh	ʌhʌ

NPA CODING SHEET

Shriberg and Kwiatkowski
John Wiley & Sons   Copyright 1980 NPA

Child: **Jack**   DOB _____   Age **5-10**

Sampling _____   Analysis _____

Date _____   Date _____

Clinician _____

Coding Sheet: [A] Nasals; Glides; Liquids

Page No. **1**

Total Words Entered **32**

Sounds: [m, n, ŋ, w, j, l, r]

	1 CV Gloss	Trans.	Code	**2 VC** Gloss	Trans.	Code	**3 CVC** Gloss	Trans.	Code	**4 c^n v(C)** Gloss	Trans.	Code	**5 (C)vc^n** Gloss	Trans.	Code	**6 Two-Syllable** Gloss	Trans.	Code	**7 Three⁺ Syllable** Gloss	Trans.	Code
m	⁷my	maɪ	C				⁷mom	mam	C							²³many	mɛni	C	¹¹umbrella	ʌmbwɛlə	C
	⁷me	mi	C				⁴³time	taɪm	C							³³match·day	mæbɔ	C			
																³⁷empty	ɛmpi	C			
																³⁸making	meɪkɪŋ	C			
n	²not	no	C	¹⁰on	ɒn	C	¹John	dʒɒn	S|C							¹³only	oʊni	C			
				²⁶in	ɪn	C	⁴rain	weɪn	LS|C							²⁴number	nʌmɛ	C			
							¹⁴when	wɛn	C												
							¹⁶me	wʌn	C												
ŋ							¹⁶thing	tɪŋ	S|C												
w	⁴²we	wi	C													¹⁵winter	wɪnɛ	C			
j	²⁶you	ju	C																		
l				³²all	ɔ	FCD										⁴⁸little	wɪdi	C			
r				³⁷are	aʊ	FCD	¹²wear	fwɛr	C|C							¹⁰rain·cat	weɪntot	C			
							¹⁶for	hʌ	FCD							²¹rain·trot(s)	weɪnbʌt	C			
							²¹pair	pɛ	C|FCD							³⁹repeat	wipit	C			
							³³car	kɔ	C|FCD												

NPA CODING SHEET

Shriberg and Kwiatkowski
John Wiley & Sons   Copyright 1980 NPA

Child Jack   DOB 5-10   Age 5-10

Sampling _____ Analysis _____ Date _____

Clinician _____

Sound	1 CV Gloss	Trans.	Code	2 VC Gloss	Trans.	Code	3 CVC Gloss	Trans.	Code	4 Cⁿ V(C) Gloss	Trans.	Code	5 (C)VCⁿ Gloss	Trans.	Code	6 Two-Syllable Gloss	Trans.	Code	7 Three⁺ Syllable Gloss	Trans.	Code
p				¹⁵ up	ʌp	C	³⁷ type	taɪ	C FCD							¹⁵ pretty	wɪdi	C			
							³⁸ keep	hi	FCD							¹⁸ open	oʊpən	C			
																¹⁸ presents	wɛʌn	C			
b	²⁴ by	baɪ	C							³⁰ blow	gwo	CR				²³ about	əbaʊ	C			
																³¹ morning	wodi	C			
t	⁵ to	tu	C	³² it	I	FCD	⁶ not	na	C FCD	⁴³ train	weɪŋ	CR C	⁷ won't	woɚn	C CR						
				¹¹ out	aʊ	FCD	⁷ lot	wɛ	LS FCD				¹² don't	dɔɚ	C CR						
							¹⁸ put	tʊt	RA C				⁴⁰ went	wɛn	C CR						
							¹⁴ hat	hat	C C												
							²⁶ write	waɪt	LS C												
							⁴⁶ got	dɔt	VF C												
							⁵⁰ gate	deɪ	VF FCD												
d							³¹ dad	dæ	C FCD				³⁷ filled(ed)	hi	CR	³ dunno	dʌnoʊ	C			
							⁴⁶ ride	waɪ	LS FCD							³⁸ different	dɪpə	C			
k							⁴ like	waɪk	LS C							¹⁵ coming	hʌmɪŋ	C			
							¹¹ take	teɪk	C C							²² candle	tænə	C			
							²³ cake	teɪk	VF C												
g	¹² go	do	VF													⁴ gonna	tunə	C			
																⁴⁰ green bay	grinbeɪ	C			

NPA CODING SHEET

Shriberg and Kwiatkowski
John Wiley & Sons   Copyright 1980 NPA

Child _Jack_ DOB _____ Age _5-10_
Sampling Date _____ Analysis Date _____
Clinician _____

Coding Sheet: [C] Fricatives; Affricates
Page No. _1_
Total Words Entered _24_
Sounds: [h, f, v, θ, ð, s, z, ʃ, ʒ, tʃ, dʒ]

Sound	1 CV Gloss	Trans.	Code	2 VC Gloss	Trans.	Code	3 CVC Gloss	Trans.	Code	4 Cⁿ V(C) Gloss	Trans.	Code	5 (C)VCⁿ Gloss	Trans.	Code	6 Two-Syllable Gloss	Trans.	Code	7 Three⁺ Syllable Gloss	Trans.	Code
h	⁵¹he	hi	C													⁴¹hotel	hotev	C			
f																					
v							¹³have	hæ	C FCD												
θ																					
ð	²⁶the	tʌ	S													³⁷other(s)	ʌðʌ v ð	C			
	⁵⁸they	do	S																		
s							²³this	dɪt	S S	⁴¹stay	teɪ	CR	⁴¹looks	fwʊʃ	CR	⁴⁴sweaty	wedi	c			
										⁴⁹stop	dap	CR c	¹²boots	bu	c	¹⁶some-time	tʌmtaɪn	c			
													²⁴six	hɪk	CR	⁴³station	teɪntɪn	c			
													³¹takes	keɪ	CR						
													³⁴lots	wɔt	CR						
													³⁵sorts	tɔrt	CR						
													³⁴cakes	kɔ	CR						
													³⁵kindle	taɪn	CR						
													⁴⁹times	taɪm c	CR						
z							⁵¹canoe	tɔ	VF FCD												
							⁵¹was	wʌ	C FCD												
ʃ																					
ʒ																					
tʃ							⁶much	mʌ	C FCD												
dʒ																					

NPA SUMMARY SHEET

Shriberg and Kwiatkowski
John Wiley & Sons   Copyright 1980 NPA

Child __Jack__   DOB __5-10__
Sampling Date ____   Age ____ Analysis ____ Date ____
Clinician ____

Total Words Entered (A+B+C) __93__

Phonetic Inventory

	m	n	ŋ	w	j	p	b	t	d	k	g	h	f	v	θ	ð	s	z	ʃ	ʒ	tʃ	dʒ	l	r
Correct Anywhere →	x	x	x	x	x	x	x	x	x	x	x	x												x
Appears Anywhere →												x												
Glossed Never Correct → Never Appears													x	x	x	x	x	x	x		x	x	x	
Never Glossed; Never Appears →																				x	x	x		

1. Final Consonant Deletion

m	n	ŋ	w	j	p	b	t	d	k	g	h	f	v	θ	ð	s	z	ʃ	ʒ	tʃ	dʒ	l	r
O	O		O		∅	-	✓	O	-	-		✓	-	-	O	✓	-	-	-	✓	-	✓	∅

2. Velar Fronting

	Initial →	Final →
	∅	O
	✓	-

3. Stopping

	Initial →	Final →

4. Palatal Fronting

	Initial →	Final →
	O	-
	-	O
	✓	✓
	O	O

5. Liquid Simplification

✓	✓
O	O

6.

Progressive Assimilations	Regressive Assimilations
none	t/p ← t

7. Cluster Reduction

	Correct	Reduced
Initial Clusters →	none	t/st gw/bl w/tr d/st k/ks ∅/ts ∅/rz n/nt f/ks t/ts n/ndz ∅/nt ∅/ks rt/rts m/mz ∅/ld
Final Clusters →	none	

8. Unstressed Syllable Deletion

	Two Syllable	Three+ Syllable
n Deletions	27	1
% Deletions	O	O
	O	O

Notes:

1. Some process data based on only one word.
2. Consider regressive assimilation - [keɪ] for "take(s)"
3. Velopharyngeal adequacy should be assessed : ɡ nasalizes all vowels ; some glottal stops noted ; /h/ substitutions for fricatives ; no correct nasal-stop clusters.

PART III

Guidelines for Interpretation and Additional Analyses

Introduction

Completion of the Phonetic Inventory and Processes sections of the Summary Sheet yields a description of the child's consonant inventory and a summary of the child's use of eight natural processes in continuous speech. Data in these 164 boxes provide a reliable index for all measurement operations, such as for assessing progress in a management program. For a more complete understanding of a child's phonology, however, analyses of data on the Transcription Sheets and Coding Sheets should be pursued. Indeed, the primary motivation for taking the time to complete the Transcription Sheets and Coding Sheets is to allow for detailed inspection of the continuous speech data.

These guidelines for interpretation of NPA results and additional analyses are divided into two subsections: (1) discussion of the three types of sound change which are found in children's speech and (2) guidelines for phonetic and process analyses of these sound changes as sampled by NPA procedures. Part IV provides four case studies that illustrate clinical applications of these analyses including suggestions for management programming.

Three Types of Sound Change

We began this text with an introduction to the concept of sound change. We said that the cover term *sound change* encompasses . . . all changes in the production of sounds, such as those that occur in a language over time; when one dialect comes in contact with another; under different speaking conditions; as slips of the tongue; as a child acquires speech, and in other phonological domains. For clinical purposes, we find it useful to separate children's sound changes into three basic classifications or types.

1. Context-Sensitive Modifications.
2. Context-Free Modifications.
3. Phoneme Deletions and Substitutions.

Not all phonologists would agree with this three-way division. Let us define each type of sound change and illustrate the role it plays in a phonological analysis.*

1. Context-Sensitive Modifications

Context-sensitive modifications include two subtypes of sound change which normally occur in the speech of children and adults in certain contexts: (a) allophones, and (b) casual or fast speech changes.

a. Allophones

Allophones are normal changes or modifications that occur as a phoneme is articulated in different syllable positions and different phonetic contexts. For example, MacKay (1978, p. 179) gives the following list of allophones for the /t/ phoneme in English.

[t⁼]	unaspirated /t/	s<u>t</u>op
[tʰ]	aspirated /t/	<u>t</u>op
[t⁷]	unreleased /t/	bough<u>t</u> two
[ɾ]	flapped /t/	bu<u>tt</u>er
[tᴺ]	nasally released /t/	bu<u>tt</u>on
[tˡ]	laterally released /t/	li<u>tt</u>le
[t̪]	dental /t/	both <u>T</u>om and I
[t̠]	back (alveolopalatal) /t/	mea<u>t</u>shop

Some of these allophones reflect speech production constraints, whereas others reflect rule-bound changes of English phonology (see Ladefoged, 1975 for an instructive discussion of allophones). The point here is that allophone-level sound changes are not articulation "errors." Rather, they are the normal variants of the abstract phoneme which are produced when their respective phonetic context conditions are met. For example, a child who says [wʊɫ] "wool" has not misarticulated /l/. A velarized /l/, [ɫ] (dark "l") in postvocalic position, as discussed on page 30, is the English allophone that occurs for /l/ in this position in normal adult speech.

b. Casual and Fast Speech Modifications

Casual and fast speech sound changes, the second type of context-sensitive modifications, occur only when the speaker is speaking in a casual (informal) register or speaking rapidly. For example, "all of them" said casually or rapidly might become [ɑləðəm]; "miss you" in casual or fast speech often becomes [mɪʃu]. Like allophones, these sound changes are not articulation errors—they are normal and predictable sound changes in casual or fast speech. If the gloss on the Transcription Sheet has appropriately allowed for these casual forms, they will not be incorrectly coded as sound changes. As suggested on page 33, words like "and" [n̩], for example, should not be chosen to enter on the Coding Sheets because to code [n̩] as Cluster Reduction would be to penalize the child for doing precisely what adults do in casual speech.

These two types of context-sensitive sound modifications—allophones and casual/fast speech changes—will occur frequently on Transcription Sheets. The point to emphasize here is that sound changes of both types are normal—in fact, they give

---

* Dialectical variants of General American speech are not sound changes as described here. The clinician must be thoroughly familiar with the dialect of a child's linguistic community in order to describe any sound changes from that dialect.

evidence that a child who uses them is learning the adult phonology. These types of changes are the rule in speech samples in which a child is encouraged to talk in a casual register, as opposed to the more formal register used in reading or single-word articulation tests. For diagnostic purposes, such as assessing the integrity of the speech mechanism at different rates of speech, careful transcription of such changes can be revealing. Examples will be provided in the case studies.

2. Context-Free Modifications

Context-free modifications differ from context-sensitive modifications in two ways: (1) They *do not* normally occur as allophones of the phoneme in the child's dialect; and (2) they *do not* normally occur when adults or children talk casually or rapidly. Context-free modifications include all sound changes that traditionally are termed articulation "distortions." With some children, we use the following set of terms and diacritics to transcribe both context-sensitive modifications and context-free modifications.*

Diacritic Symbols Used Frequently in NPA Transcription

[ˌ]	dentalized	for sibilants and alveolars /t/, /d/, /n/, /l/ articulated with the tongue tip too far forward
[ˏ]	lateralized	for sibilants in which the air stream is emitted laterally
[ˌ]	palatalized	for sibilants in which the tongue is flattened, rather than grooved
[ˌ]	retroflexed	for sibilants in which the tongue tip is curled back
[_]	derhotacized	for /r/ sounds with reduced r-coloring: [ɪ], [ɝ], [ɚ]
[˷]	velarized	for /r/ and /l/ in which the blade of the tongue approximates the velum
[˜]	nasalized	for vowels with nasal resonance
[﹡]	denasalized	for vowels with denasal resonance
[ː]	lengthened	for vowels that are longer in duration
[ʰ]	aspirated	for stops in which the release is followed by a burst of air
[⁼]	unaspirated	for stops in which the release is not followed by a burst of air
[ˈ]	weak release	for stops in which the release is slower and/or less intense

* Narrow phonetic transcription of this type is used only for children with severe delays (see for example, Case Study #3), or for special inquiry purposes.

These diacritics and others (Shriberg & Kent, in preparation) usually are used only to indicate sound changes that are not predicted by context, that is, only for context-free sound changes. For example, if a child uses a velarized /l/, [ɫ] in *prevocalic* position ([ɫæmp] for "lamp"), we use the velarized diacritic to indicate this modification; however, when /l/ is normally velarized as in the earlier example of [wʊɫ] "wool," we may omit the diacritic. Similarly, /p/ is normally aspirated in prevocalic position, so we usually do not transcribe the aspiration (for example, [pɪt] "pit"). When aspiration occurs where an *unaspirated* allophone should normally occur, however (for example, [spʰɪt] for "spit") we may elect to indicate the aspiration. Another example: If a child nasalizes a vowel in a non-nasal context [bĩd] for "bead," we usually would use the nasalization diacritic to capture this interesting modification; in contexts where assimilative nasality is predictable, for example, [min] "mean," we may not use the nasality diacritic.

Context-free modifications, then, are slight to pronounced sound changes that occur in contexts that would not ordinarily be associated with such changes. Whether or not deviations from standard speech, such as [ʂ], [s̺], or [ɹ], are "handicapping" is, of course, outside of the matter of transcription. The transcription task is to capture faithfully, the precise place/manner features of a child's speech sound modifications. In the guidelines that follow and in the case examples, we discuss how such sound changes are viewed for diagnostic and management purposes.

3. Phoneme Deletions and Substitutions

The third major type of sound change includes two subtypes: (a) natural processes and (b) uncoded deletions and substitutions.

a. Natural Processes

As developed earlier, the NPA procedure assumes a small set of natural processes that (1) are attested in the phonological literature, (2) can be transcribed reliably in the clinical situation, and (3) are seen frequently among children with delayed speech. Among the eight natural processes included in the NPA, three involve phoneme deletions (Final Consonant Deletion, Cluster Reduction, Unstressed Syllable Deletion) and five involve substitution of phonemes (Stopping, Liquid Simplification, Velar Fronting, Palatal Fronting, and Assimilation). As developed in the guidelines to follow, the presumption is that these deletions and substitutions occur for one of two reasons. Either the sound is not "available" in the child's phonetic inventory (which itself, of course, requires explanation) or the sound is available, but the difficulty of the canonical form or some other factor requires that a simplification process operate on the sound. As described next in these guidelines, a *Phonetic Analysis* allows the clinician to determine which of these two possibilities best reflects the data. If a sound in fact, is determined to be in a child's phonetic inventory, then the *Process Analysis* seeks to determine what aspects of a child's phonological system underlie deletion or replacement of the sound.

b. Uncoded Deletions and Substitutions

A second type of deletion or substitution sound change appears on the NPA Coding Sheets as either a deletion symbol [ø], or the box is simply left blank. What factors underlie such sound changes? For example, if a child deletes the first consonant in a word, what are we to make of it diagnostically? Words usually are not simplified in this way. Or for example, of what diagnostic significance is it if a child substitutes a glide for a fricative? Again, some of these particular deletions and substitutions *may* be extensions of normal development, that is, natural simplifications. In this procedure, we simply do not view them that way.* Until reliable data warrant an alternative procedure, we think it best to leave all substitutions and deletions other than those described in the basic set of eight natural processes as "uncoded" (the boxes on the Coding Sheets are left blank).

Summary

In summary, we have divided the sound changes that occur in children's continuous speech into three types as follows.

Type 1	Type 2	Type 3
Context-Sensitive Modifications	Context-Free Modifications	Phoneme Deletions and Substitutions
(a) Allophones (b) Casual and Fast Speech Changes	All place/manner changes that do not qualify as Type 1 modifications	(a) Natural Processes (b) Uncoded Deletions and Substitutions

We have said that context-sensitive modifications (Type 1) are not considered articulation "errors," whereas context-free modifications (Type 2) and phoneme deletions and substitutions (Type 3) *are* viewed as errors, depending on the age of the child (see Appendix A) and on current definitions of handicap (see Shriberg, 1980). These concepts of sound change are basic to the guidelines for Phonetic Analysis and Process Analysis that follow. Phonetic Analysis is concerned with description of context-sensitive modifications, context-free modifications, and uncodable deletions and substitutions. Process Analysis, in turn, is concerned with identifying which processes a child uses, identifying which stage of process dissolution best characterizes those processes a child uses, and identifying which linguistic contexts, if any, are associated with process usage.

Phonetic Analysis

Information from a phonetic analysis is important diagnostically and is basic to an understanding of the natural process data. The clinician has the opportunity to inspect all sources—the Transcription Sheets, the Coding Sheets, and the Summary Sheet—to

---

* For example, substitutions such as [f/θ], [s/θ], and [θ/s] will be "uncoded." Whether or not such changes within manner are as "natural" as stopping of fricatives—questions that require further study—these sound changes are left uncoded in the basic procedure. Certainly [s/θ] and [θ/s] can not *both* be natural processes, because simplifications can not be bidirectional!

provide answers to two questions: (1) What articulatory features are present in the child's inventory of correct sounds, and how do these compare to normative data? and (2) What context-sensitive modifications (Type 1), context-free modifications (Type 2), or uncodable deletions and substitutions (Type 3a) are present in the sample?

1. What Articulatory Features Are Present in the Child's Inventory of Sounds and How Do These Compare to Normative Data?

Development of sounds within place-manner classes is described in Appendix A. It is important to keep in mind that recent studies (Hare & Irwin, 1978; Prather et al., 1975) indicate that children "master" these features at younger ages than reflected in the classical studies of speech sound development (as summarized by Sander, 1972). Notice too that NPA data sample a child's articulation of sounds in continuous speech, not in citation test forms as used in most normative studies. Furthermore, response definitions for "correct" sounds as given in this text are different from those used in all other studies. That is, we do not view certain types of modifications (for example, a dentalized /s/, [s̪]) as meeting criteria for being coded as a process. For these and other reasons, the phonetic inventory data as recorded on a child's Summary Sheet may not directly be comparable to even recent normative data. Phonetic transcription of the child's speech as recorded on the Transcription Sheets is the best source of phonetic information, but again, these continuous speech data will differ from production in isolated words (Faircloth & Faircloth, 1970).

With these constraints in mind, the Transcription Sheets and the Summary Sheet should be inspected carefully to determine which features the child *does use* in continuous speech. That is, which of the six manner classes—nasals, stops, fricatives, affricates, glides, and liquids—are "available" in the child's inventory of speech sounds. Notice that the Summary Sheet groups sounds by manner features, with place features nested from the front to the back of the vocal tract within each manner class (except /h/). Careful inspection of the *first two rows* on the Summary Sheet then, indicates which sounds the child says correctly in at least one instance and which sounds are said as replacements for other sounds. Where narrow phonetic transcription has been used, analyses should include reference to the transcription data. These data are important for interpreting phonological processes and formulating intervention approaches, as will be illustrated in the case studies.

2. What Is the Nature of the Sound Changes That Are Evident in the Sample?

As important as knowing what the child says correctly—as sought in answering the question above—is precise description of the types of sound changes the child uses. For this question about the child's phonetic inventory we employ the concepts just presented about the three major types of sound change. The clinician is interested in which of the "distortion" sound changes are context-sensitive modifications versus context-free modifications, and which of the deletions and substitutions are either a natural process or "uncodable." Here are some examples.

a. If nasalized vowels are seen on the Transcription Sheets, do they occur only in nasal contexts, for example, "banana," or do they occur in non-nasal contexts, for example, "read?" The first possibility satisfies criteria for a Type 1 sound change (context-sensitive modification); the second is viewed as Type 2 sound change (context-free modification).

b. If a dentalized /s/, [s̪], occurs in the sample, is the context one in which slight dentalization of /s/ might be expected, for example, following /t/, [ts̪] (Type 1) or is the modification in a context where dentalization would not be expected (a Type 2 sound change, context-free modification)?

c. If a substitution or deletion is recorded, is there a natural process that describes the error (for example, /s/→[t] = Stopping), or is the sound change "uncodable" by the criteria for coding listed in this text (for example, /w/→[k] = ?).

Illustrations of phonetic inventory analyses that integrate these questions are provided in the case studies. To make the point here, however, let us use a previous example to show how these two phonetic analyses questions are pursued. In the sample Summary Sheet for Jack (page 57) we wrote in the *Notes* section:

Velopharyngeal adequacy should be assessed: J. nasalizes all vowels; some glottal stops noted; /h/ substitutions for fricatives; no correct nasal stop clusters.

In fact, the oral peripheral examination and subsequent instrumental analyses did suggest marginal velopharyngeal insufficiency. Note how Jack's sound change data include errors that are not accounted for by natural processes.

a. Hypernasality occurs in non-nasal environments = a Type 2 sound change.

b. Glottal stops were used to replace other stops = an uncodable substitution; a Type 3b sound change.

c. /h/ substitutions for other fricatives = an uncodable substitution; a Type 3b sound change.

d. No correct nasal-stop clusters = a Type 3a sound change, typical of the very earliest stage of cluster acquisition (see Appendix A) and hence inconsistent with Jack's correct production of other clusters.

Some of Jack's speech sound changes are "natural" in the sense defined in this text, while the changes above are not natural. These four essentially independent pieces of linguistic data implicate the velopharyngeal mechanism.

This example illustrates the value of careful phonetic analysis. Differential diagnosis of children with delayed speech is a major responsibility of the clinician. Jack had been viewed as a child with speech delay of unknown origin before our analysis. His overall complex pattern of sound changes evidently had masked a component specifically related to velopharyngeal functioning.

Process Analysis

A child's phonetic-level behaviors, those that are both present and absent in the continuous speech sample, have been described. The remaining sound changes are those considered natural processes (that is, the Type 3a changes). The two questions to be addressed are: (1) For each of the natural processes a child uses at least some of the time, at what developmental stage is the child functioning? and (2) What context/function variables are associated with "inconsistent" process use?

1. For Each of the Natural Processes a Child Uses at Least Some of the Time, at What Developmental Stage Is the Child Functioning?

Developmental data for each of the eight NPA processes and other putative "natural" processes are provided in Appendix A. It is important to underscore the tentative nature of current normative information in phonology. Data summarized in Appendix A will require updating as the results of current large-scale studies of child phonology become available. Hopefully, contemporary studies will provide reliable normative data on the routes children take in acquiring the phonological component of the grammar. Most attractive, particularly from the point of view of assessment, is the notion that reliable process stage data will emerge for children with delayed speech. For example, consider development of the cluster [br]. For just this cluster alone, a child might say: [br], [b], [r], [r] (derhotacized) [bw], [w], or something else. Each of these behaviors could indicate a level of functioning of the phonological stage of stop-liquid cluster development. Reliance on developmental data, of course, is at the heart of the developmental approach to assessment, prediction, and management of children with speech and language delays. Although both children with normally developing speech and children with delayed speech show large individual differences *across* process usage, stage data *within* each process is reasonable to expect (because it should mirror phonetic development).

The procedures for a process stage analysis are quite straightforward. The Coding Sheets and Summary Sheet were expressly set up to provide a convenient grouping of sounds by processes and canonical structure. Using whatever data are available in Appendix A (updated as warranted by emerging literature), the clinician selects the stage that best characterizes the child's current phonology. For example, Final Consonant Deletion is assumed to have 10 stages; for the child in question, the task is to determine which stage best matches the data available from the NPA sheets. Examples of process stage analyses are provided in the case studies.

2. What Context/Function Variables Are Associated with Inconsistent Process Use?

An important constraint on the formal aspects of the NPA procedure is that only one token of each word appearing on the Transcription Sheets is used. If a child says a word incorrectly the first time, but later says it correctly, for example, only the first, incorrect word is used. Although this was an efficient solution from a testing viewpoint, some recourse to *all* the data should be available. This is the place in the NPA procedure where all such variability can be dealt with productively. The goal is to determine if variable use of any process is actually consistent. That is, can variability of performance be traced to certain *context* (structural) variables, to syntactic-semantic-pragmatic *function* variables, or to a combination of these variables?

Procedures for a context/function analysis can range from a simple "eyeball" approach—a scan of the transcripts to look for variables associated with process use—to quantified worksheet tabulations. Like other choice points in the NPA procedures, the particulars of the situation will determine how much attention should be given to consistency analyses. A context/function analysis is illustrated in two of the case studies. Here we present some general guidelines for a worksheet approach.

Step 1

Eyeball the data on the Transcription Sheets and Coding Sheets to see if any data seem "inconsistent." That is, do any of the processes used only "Sometimes" seem to vary as a function of the linguistic context or the linguistic function of the lexical item? Here are just some of the possible context and function variables that could be associated with use of a process.

Context Variables—Are any of These Variables Associated with Process Use?

Canonical form:	CV versus VC versus VCV and so forth.
Position in word:	Initial versus medial versus final and so forth.
Phonetic context:	What sounds are adjacent to or near the target sound.
Length of word:	Monosyllable versus two-syllable, versus three-syllable, and so forth.
Stress:	What is the stress assignment of the lexical item—primary stress versus secondary stress and so forth.
Rate:	What was the child's rate of speech for the target segment, and so forth.

Function Variables—Are any of These Variables Associated with Process Use?

Syntactic function:	What syntactic function does the lexical item have.
Semantic function:	What semantic function does the lexical item have.
Pragmatic function:	What pragmatic function does the lexical item have.

These general categories are only to indicate the difference between context variables, which include structural aspects of the lexical item in context, and functional variables, which refer to the *function* of the item in the grammar. Miller (1980) describes a number of procedures for coding lexical items into their syntactic, semantic, and pragmatic functions.

Step 2

Set up sectors on a worksheet which subdivide the child's performance on each target process into correct versus incorrect productions. For example, if the analysis seeks to determine whether the child's inconsistent use of Final Consonant Deletion is actually patterned in some way by the context or function of words, subdivide the page with half for Final Consonant Deletion entries and half for words in which the final consonant was not deleted. Then go through the transcript and enter in each half of the worksheet, respectively, utterances that contain words in which final consonants were and were not deleted. Depending on what context/function variables might be associated with differential use of the process, the whole utterance, or just a few words adjacent to the target word might be entered.

Step 3

With the data thus arranged on the worksheet, any association between column variables and row divisions should be apparent. Simple tabulations and perhaps percentages should indicate whether or not inconsistent use of a process is actually related to linguistic context or linguistic function variables. Notice that this procedure makes use of all the data stored on the Transcription Sheets. As before, the time needed to complete NPA analyses of continuous speech is well spent if such analyses are productive. The case studies that follow illustrate only some sample approaches to describing a child's phonological system in a way that has immediate clinical utility.

Review and Discussion Questions

1. Define the following types of sound changes and describe their role in diagnosis, prediction, and management of children with delayed speech development (61 to 65).

   a. *Type 1:* Context-Sensitive Modifications
      Allophones.
      Casual and fast speech changes.

   b. *Type 2:* Context-Free Modifications

   c. *Type 3:* Phoneme Deletions and Substitutions
      Natural processes.
      Uncoded deletions and substitutions.

2. Describe the two types of descriptive data that are obtained in a Phonetic Analysis (65 to 67).

3. Describe the concept of *developmental stage* as it applies to NPA analysis, prediction, and management (68).

4. Describe the concept of *context/function analysis* and procedures you would use to analyze a natural process used inconsistently by a child (68).

PART IV

Case Studies

To this point in the text we have presented theoretical background and the "nuts and bolts" of natural process analyses and additional analyses. In this section we consolidate and elaborate these materials in the form of four case studies. In our experience with upwards of 100 analyses of the type to be presented here, plus many more done by student clinicians, we have found that each child will have unique phonetic/phonological features that can be isolated by careful application of NPA procedures. The case studies presented in this section have been selected to provide a glimpse at this diversity among children with delayed speech. Close study and discussion of these case studies should allow students to grasp firmly the utility of NPA descriptions in diagnosis and management planning.

Case Study 1: Robby

Brief Case History

Robby was seven years, one month old when referred to our clinic. He was rated by his clinician as moderately unintelligible to person's meeting him for the first time. Robby's cognitive development and language comprehension were essentially age appropriate, but vocabulary and other productive language indices were delayed approximately one year. His early developmental history was unremarkable, with the exception of very frequent colds with possibly fluctuating hearing loss. Robby had been receiving speech and language services twice weekly in the public schools for two years. His clinician reported steady progress in both speech and language acquisition. However, Robby was viewed as an "easily distractible" child. He had been referred to a summer phonology clinic for the opportunity to have intensive speech-language services.

NPA Analysis

NPA Data Sheets

The following pages are the completed NPA data sheets. Interpretation and additional analyses begin on page 85).

Child __Robby__   DOB __7-1__
Sampling ____ Age ____ Analysis
Date ____ Date ____
Clinician ____

NPA TRANSCRIPTION SHEET
Shriberg and Kwiatkowski   Copyright 1980 NPA
John Wiley & Sons

Comments on
Sample
Conditions

Item No.	GLOSS	TRANSCRIPTION
1	good	gʊd
2	cupcake	kʌpkeɪk
3	ice cream	aɪ krim
4	chocolate	bɔklɛt
5	everyday	ɛvrɪdeɪ
6	and once (im) awhile	æn wʌnt ahwaɪl
7	we're going at my sister(s) camp	wir goɪn æt maɪ tɪtə kæmp
8	long way	lɛm uɪ
9	two more day(s)	du mɔr deɪ
10	Indiana	ɪndɪænə

Item No.	GLOSS	TRANSCRIPTION
11	we him there before	wi bɪn ʃeɪr bɔr
12	soccer	tako
13	oh yeah	o jæ
14	I get nine	aɪ gɛt naɪn
15	I can	aɪ kæn
16	seven	tɛbɪn
17	no	no
18	Disneyworld	dɪsɪnwɔrp
19	Mickey Mouse	mɪki maʊt
20	play	pleɪ

Child Patty DOB ___ Age 7-1
Sampling ___ Analysis ___
Date ___ Date ___
Clinician ___

NPA TRANSCRIPTION SHEET
Shriberg and Kwiatkowski
John Wiley & Sons   Copyright 1980 NPA

Page No. 2
Comments on Sample Conditions

Item No.	GLOSS	TRANSCRIPTION	Item No.	GLOSS	TRANSCRIPTION
21	Donald Duck	danəld dʌk	31	big seat	bɪg dit
22	cake	keɪk	32	brother	brʌdɔ
23	chocolate	dɔklɛt	33	sister	tɪtɔ
24	golf	galp	34	three people can sit in front	pi pipəl kæn pit ɪn pʌnt
25	point	pɔnt	35	sometime	tʌmtaɪm
26	one time I bring my big wheel	wʌn taɪm aɪ brɪŋ maɪ bɪg hwil	36	please	plid
27	bring that in car	bwɪŋ dæt ɪn kɔr	37	we got (two) thing	wi gat tu dɪŋ
28	in the front	ɪn də pʌnt	38	one on top	wʌn an tap
29	in the back	ɪn də bæk	39	picking her up	pɪkɪŋ hɔ ʌp
30	my mom and my dad driving	maɪ mam æn maɪ dæd graɪvɪŋ	40	sleeping five day(s)	lipɪŋ paɪ deɪ

Child Betty   DOB _____   Age 7-1

Sampling _____   Analysis _____

Date _____   Date _____

Clinician _____

NPA TRANSCRIPTION SHEET
Shriberg and Kwiatkowski
John Wiley & Sons   Copyright 1980 NPA

Comments on
Sample _____
Conditions _____

Item No.	GLOSS	TRANSCRIPTION	Item No.	GLOSS	TRANSCRIPTION
41	hotel	otɛl	51	putting some	pʌtɪŋ dʌm
42 →	I got my own drippy	ai gat mai on nupi	52	cement	tɪmɛnt
43	put a lock on the	pʌt eɪ lak an də	53	mailman laughing	meɪlmæn læpɪŋ
44	whistle	wɪtʌl	54	still laughing	tɪl læpɪŋ
45	dancing	dæntɪŋ	55	going round	goɪŋ raʊn
46	and (the) mail come	æn deɪ meɪl kʌm	56	wolf come(s)	wʊlp kʌm
47	mailman	meɪlmæn	57	wolf want eat them up	wʊlp wʌnt it dɛm ʌp
48	another one	anʌdə wʌn	58	mailman (hat) go up	meɪlmæn æt go ʌp
49	with the flute	wɪ də fut	59	and taking the rig in now	æn teɪkɪŋ də rʌg ɪn naʊ
50	pig	bɪg	60	huff puff	hʌp pʌp

Child _Patty_ DOB _____ Age _7-1_
Sampling _____ Analysis _____
Date _____ Date _____
Clinician _____

NPA TRANSCRIPTION SHEET

Shriberg and Kwiatkowski   Copyright 1980 NPA
John Wiley & Sons

Comments on _____
Sample _____
Conditions _____

Item No.	GLOSS	TRANSCRIPTION	Item No.	GLOSS	TRANSCRIPTION
61	blow a house down	bo ʌ haʊt daʊn			
62	look	lʊk			
63	rope	rʌp			
64	fast	bæt			

NPA CODING SHEET

Shriberg and Kwiatkowski
John Wiley & Sons   Copyright 1980 NPA

Child: Crofty DOB: _____ Age: 7-1
Sampling Date: _____ Analysis Date: _____
Clinician: _____

Sound	1 CV Gloss/Trans/Code	2 VC Gloss/Trans/Code	3 CVC Gloss/Trans/Code	4 Cⁿ V(C)	5 (C)VCⁿ	6 Two-Syllable Gloss/Trans/Code	7 Three⁺ Syllable Gloss/Trans/Code
m	⁷my maɪ C		²⁶time taɪm C|C; ³⁰mom mam C|C; ⁴⁶come kʌm C|C; ⁵¹some dam S|C			¹⁶mickey mɪki C; ⁴⁷mailman meɪlmæn C	
n	¹⁷no no C; ⁵⁴mmm naʊ C	²⁷in ɪm/ɪn C; ³⁸an ʌm/ʌn C; ⁴²on ɑʊn/ɒn C	¹¹green bin C|C; ¹⁴mine naɪn C|C; ¹⁵ran kæn C|C; ²⁶one wʌn C|C; ⁶¹down daʊn C|C				¹⁸Indiana ɪndɪænə C; ⁴⁸another anʌðə C
ŋ			⁸long lɔŋ C; ³⁷thing dɪŋ S|C				
w	⁸way weɪ C; ¹¹we wi C		³⁶wheel hwil C|C; ⁴⁶mail meɪl C			⁶awhile ahwaɪl C; ⁴⁴whistle wɪtl C	
j	¹³yeah jæ/jɒ C						
l			³⁶wheel hwil C|C; ⁴⁶mail meɪl C			⁵³laughing læpɪŋ C	
r			⁷we're wɪr C|C; ⁹more mɔr C|C; ¹¹there ðeɪr C|C; ²⁷her kɔr C|C				

NPA CODING SHEET

Shriberg and Kwiatkowski
John Wiley & Sons   Copyright 1980 NPA

Child _Robby_   DOB _7-1_
Sampling _____ Age _____ Analysis _____
Date _____   Date _____
Clinician _____

Coding Sheet: [A] Nasals; Glides; Liquids
Total Words Entered _____   Page No. _2_
Sounds: | m, n, ŋ, w, j, l, r |

Sound	1 CV			2 VC			3 CVC			4 C^n V(C)			5 (C) VC^n			6 Two-Syllable			7 Three⁺ Syllable		
	Gloss	Trans.	Code	Gloss	Trans.	Code	Gloss	Trans.	Code	Gloss	Trans.	Code	Gloss	Trans.	Code	Gloss	Trans.	Code	Gloss	Trans.	Code
m							S^7 them	dɛm	S | C												
n																					
ŋ																					
w																					
j																					
l																					
r																					

NPA CODING SHEET

Shriberg and Kwiatkowski
John Wiley & Sons   Copyright 1980 NPA

Child __Bobby__   DOB __7-1__   Age __7-1__
Sampling _____   Analysis _____
Date _____   Date _____
Clinician _____

Sound	**1** CV Gloss	Trans.	Code	**2** VC Gloss	Trans.	Code	**3** CVC Gloss	Trans.	Code	**4** Cⁿ V(C) Gloss	Trans.	Code	**5** (C) VCⁿ Gloss	Trans.	Code	**6** Two-Syllable Gloss	Trans.	Code	**7** Three⁺ Syllable Gloss	Trans.	Code
p				³⁹ up	ʌp	C	³⁸ top	tap	C C	²⁰ play	pleɪ	C	⁷ camp	kæmp	C C	³⁴ purple	pipəl	C			
										³⁶ please	plid	C S				³⁵ picking	pɪkɪŋ	C			
																⁵¹ putting	pʌtɪŋ	C			
b										⁴¹ blow	bo	CR				¹¹ before	bɔr	VSD			
										²⁴ bring	brɪŋ	C C				³² brother	brʌdɔ	C			
t	⁹ two	du	C	⁵⁷ eat	it	C	¹⁴ get	get	C C				²⁵ point	pɔnt	C C	⁵⁶ taking	teɪkɪŋ	C			
				⁷ at	æt	C	²⁷ that	dæt	S C				²⁸ front	pʌnt	CR C						
							³¹ eat	dit	S C				⁵⁷ want	wɔnt	C C						
							³⁴ sit	pɪt	S C				⁶⁴ fast	bæt	CR						
							³⁷ get	gæt	C C												
							⁴³ put	pʌt	C C												
d							¹ good	gʊd	C C				⁵⁵ round	rʌund	C CR	²⁹ Donald	danʌld	C	¹⁵ Disney- world	dɪsniwʊrld	C
							³⁰ dad	dæd	C C							³⁰ driving	graɪvɪŋ	C			
																⁴⁵ dancing	dæntɪŋ	C			
k							²¹ duck	dʌk	C C							² cupcake	kʌpkeɪk				
							²² cake	keɪk	C C												
							²⁹ back	bæk	C C												
							⁴³ lock	lak	C C												
g							²⁶ ring	rɪŋ	C C							⁷ going	goɪŋ	C			
							⁵⁰ pig	bɪg	C C												
							⁵⁹ rug	rʌg	C C												

NPA CODING SHEET

Shriberg and Kwiatkowski
John Wiley & Sons   Copyright 1980 NPA

Child _Cathy_   DOB _____   Age _1-1_
Sampling _____   Analysis _____
Date _____   Date _____
Clinician _____

Coding Sheet: [B] Stops
Page No. _2_
Total Words Entered _____
Sounds: [p, b, t, d, k, g,]

Sound	**1** CV			**2** VC			**3** CVC			**4** C^n V(C)			**5** (C) VC^n			**6** Two-Syllable			**7** Three+ Syllable		
	Gloss	Trans.	Code	Gloss	Trans.	Code	Gloss	Trans.	Code	Gloss	Trans.	Code	Gloss	Trans.	Code	Gloss	Trans.	Code	Gloss	Trans.	Code
p																					
b																					
t																					
d																					
k					"look"	luk	cic														
g																					

NPA CODING SHEET

Shriberg and Kwiatkowski
John Wiley & Sons   Copyright 1980 NPA

Child __Cathy__   DOB _____
Age __7-1__
Sampling _____   Analysis _____
Date _____   Date _____
Clinician _____

Coding Sheet: [C] Fricatives; Affricates
Page No. __1__
Total Words Entered __24__
Sounds: [h, f, v, θ, ð, s, z, ʃ, ʒ, tʃ, dʒ]

Sound	1 CV			2 VC			3 CVC			4 Cⁿ V(C)			5 (C) VCⁿ			6 Two-Syllable			7 Three⁺ Syllable		
	Gloss	Trans.	Code	Gloss	Trans.	Code	Gloss	Trans.	Code	Gloss	Trans.	Code	Gloss	Trans.	Code	Gloss	Trans.	Code	Gloss	Trans.	Code
h																⁴ hotel	otɛl	C			
f							⁶⁰ huff / ¹⁶ puff	hʌp / pɹʌp	C|S / C|S	⁴⁹ fluze	fut	CR|C									
v							⁴⁰ five	paɪ	S IFCD	⁵⁶ wolf	wʌlp	C|CR							⁵ every-day	ɛvridɛɪ	C
θ							⁴⁹ with	wɪ	C|FCD	³⁴ three	pi	CR|									
ð	²⁸ the	dʌ	S																		
s							¹⁹ mouse / ⁴ house	maʊt / haʊt	C|S / C|S	⁵⁴ still	tɪl	CR|C	⁶ once	wʌnt	C|CR	³ ice-cream	aɪkrim	C			
																⁷ yesterday	tɪtɚ	C			
																¹² soccer	taka	C			
																¹⁶ seven	tɛbɪn	C			
																³⁵ sister	tɪtɔ	C			
																³⁵ arm-time	tamtaɪm	C			
z							⁹ day(s)	deɪ	C|FCD				⁵⁴ come(s)	kʌm	C|CR						
ʃ																					
ʒ																					
tʃ																⁴ chocolate	bɔklɛt	C			
dʒ																					

NPA CODING SHEET

Shriberg and Kwiatkowski
John Wiley & Sons   Copyright 1980 NPA

Child __Cathy__

DOB __7-1__
Age __7-1__

Sampling _____ Analysis _____
Date _____ Date _____
Clinician _____

Coding Sheet: [C] Fricatives; Affricates

Page No. __4__

Total Words Entered __2__

Sounds: [h, f, v, θ, ð, s, z, ʃ, ʒ, tʃ, dʒ]

Sound	1 CV			2 VC			3 CVC			4 Cⁿ V(C)			5 (C) VCⁿ			6 Two-Syllable			7 Three⁺ Syllable		
	Gloss	Trans.	Code	Gloss	Trans.	Code	Gloss	Trans.	Code	Gloss	Trans.	Code	Gloss	Trans.	Code	Gloss	Trans.	Code	Gloss	Trans.	Code
h							⁶³ roof	rup	c S												
f																					
v																					
θ																					
ð																					
s																⁴⁰ sleeping	lipɪŋ	c			
																⁴² snappy	nupi	c			
z																⁵² cement	ti mɛnt	c			
ʃ																					
ʒ																					
tʃ																					
dʒ																					

NPA SUMMARY SHEET

Shriberg and Kwiatkowski
John Wiley & Sons   Copyright 1980 NPA

Child **Bobby**   DOB _____   Age **7-1**
Sampling Date _____   Analysis Date _____
Clinician _____

Total Words Entered (A + B + C) **105**

PROCESS SYMBOLS
- ✓ Always Occurs
- ∅ Sometimes Occurs
- ○ Never Occurs
- – No Data Available

Phonetic Inventory

	m	n	ŋ	w	j	p	b	t	d	k	g	h	f	v	θ	ð	s	z	ʃ	ʒ	tʃ	dʒ	l	r
Correct Anywhere →	x	x	x	x	x	x	x	x	x	x	x	x	x	x		x							x	x
Appears Anywhere →															x		x	x						
Glossed Never Correct; Never Appears →															x				x	x	x	x		
Never Glossed; Never Appears →																								

1 Final Consonant Deletion

m	n	ŋ	w	j	p	b	t	d	k	g	h	f	v	θ	ð	s	z	ʃ	ʒ	tʃ	dʒ	l	r
○	○	○			–	○	○	○	○	○		○	○	✓	–	○	✓	–	–	–	–	–	○

2 Velar Fronting

Initial →	○
Final →	○

3 Stopping

	f	v	θ	ð	s	z	ʃ	ʒ	tʃ	dʒ
Initial →	✓	–	✓	∅	✓	∅	✓	–	–	–
Final →	✓	○	○	–	✓	✓	–	∅	–	–

4 Palatal Fronting

	ʃ	ʒ	tʃ	dʒ
Initial →	–	–	○	○
Final →	–	–	○	○

5 Liquid Simplification

l	r

6

Progressive Assimilations	Regressive Assimilations
none	none

7 Cluster Reduction

	Correct	Reduced	
Initial Clusters →	pl br	b/bl pl/əl t/st	f/fl pl/fr
Final Clusters →	mp nt	t/st pl/f m/mz	n/nd nt/ns

8 Unstressed Syllable Deletion

	Two Syllable	Three+ Syllable
n	27	4
n Deletions	1	0
% Deletions	4	0

Notes:

see additional analysis

Phonetic Analysis

As indicated on the Summary Sheet and from the results of stimulability testing, Robby has phonetic command of all place-manner-voicing features. Nasals, stops, glides, and liquids are produced correctly. Within the fricatives, the labiodentals /f/, /v/, and the linguadental /ð/ are correct at least some of the time; sibilant fricatives /s/, /z/ were correct only once in many coded words. Data are not available for the palatal fricatives and few data are available for the affricates. Importantly, Robby does not have any context-free or context-sensitive distortions. Stimulability testing indicates that he produces sibilant fricative /s/, /z/ in isolation with minimal auditory-visual modeling.

Overall, Robby's sound changes appear to be associated more with phonological processes—that is, with deletions and substitutions—than with phonetic-level distortions. His speech mechanism control, including tongue placement accuracy, is entirely adequate.

Process Analysis

On the basis of the available coded data, Robby's phonological sound changes essentially are limited to three processes: (1) Final Consonant Deletion, (2) Stopping, and (3) Cluster Reduction. The developmental stage picture is as follows.

1. Final Consonant Deletion

Robby is at Stage 8/Stage 9 of Renfrew's (1966) observed 10 stages of final consonant acquisition in children with delayed speech (see Appendix A). Out of 43 CVC words on the Coding Sheet, only three (7 percent) were reduced by Final Consonant Deletion. These data indicate that FCD is in the process of dissolution and does not require management.

2. Stopping

Robby is at Stage 1/Stage 2 of the five stages of fricative/affricate development (see Appendix A) proposed by Ingram (1976). He either stops or deletes fricatives most of the time, depending on whether a sound is in his phonetic inventory and its position in the word (initial versus final). Initial fricatives are always replaced by stops; final fricatives may be correct, deleted, or replaced by stops. As will be suggested, Stopping is the one process that should be targeted for management programming.

3. Cluster Reduction

Robby is at Stage 3 of the four stages of cluster acquisition (see Appendix A). With the exception of a few reduced nasal-stop and stop-liquid clusters (each of which is balanced by correct clusters of the voiced-voiceless cognate), Cluster Reductions are limited to Stopping or deletions of fricatives. Deletion versus Stopping of fricatives, again, follows the earlier description of Robby's phonetic inventory and the FCD and Stopping data. Sounds barely entering his phonetic inventory such as [f] are sometimes correct in fricative-liquid clusters—for example, [f/fl]—but, sometimes they are stopped, for example, [p/fr]. Sounds that Robby never says correctly in singletons, for example /s/, /z/, are either deleted [t/st], or stopped [nt/ns].

Eyeballing the data on the Transcription Sheets there is no indication that context-function analyses would be productive. Analyses to this point indicate that Robby's sound changes are specifically focused on fricative and affricate production. On the three grammatical morphemes in the sample "days," "comes," and "sisters," Robby deletes or stops the /s/ or /z/. Notice, however, that deletion and Stopping occur also when /s/ in word-final position does not function as a grammatical morpheme.

Implications of NPA Data for Management Programming

These analyses indicate that fricative production is the source of most of Robby's sound change errors. His production of liquids is normal and he has not developed distortions of fricatives. A management program that focuses directly on fricative production is indicated; the following programming elements should be considered.

1. Because Robby is stimulable on fricatives, the emphasis should be on "when to" articulate a fricative, rather than on "how to" articulate a fricative (Shriberg, 1980). That is, response development procedures should stabilize the fricative feature as contrasted to stops, rather than spending time on perfecting Robby's production of fricatives.

2. The /s/ and /z/ sounds should be excellent to teach in clusters. Sequencing decisions center on the following choices.

Should /s/ or /z/ be taught first in word-initial position or taught first in word-final position?

Should fricatives be taught in singletons or in clusters?

Should fricatives be taught only as word-initial or word-final sounds or should they be taught as they function in several grammatical morphemes (for example, plural, possessive, copula)?

Experimental data on such programming decisions presently are unavailable. Some developmental acoustic data would support teaching /s/ in the final position first and stress the use of /s/ clusters. Morphophonemic use of /s/ would require, of course, that the child was at an appropriate stage of language development (Paul & Shriberg, 1979). Hodson (1978) suggests teaching fricative clusters first because they include both the child's new and old sound. That is, a final cluster such as /ts/ contains both /t/—the sound that formerly replaced /s/ for a child who stops fricatives—and /s/. Final clusters that have morphophonemic function are attractive because they allow the clinician to program for both syntactic and phonological goals. Clusters involving /s/ are used in over 70 percent of the 14 grammatical morphemes; making these elements available to a child promotes expansion of language development at many levels, including lexical development. Robby, in fact, was placed on an experimental version of an /s/ Morpheme Program (Shriberg & Kwiatkowski, in submission) and his progress was excellent.

3. Because Robby does not, for example, front velars, or reduce syllables, the words in which /s/ and /z/ are taught do not have to be controlled for the possible influences of other processes. As discussed in detail elsewhere (Shriberg & Kwiatkowski, in submission), natural process data are useful for both target response selection in a management program and for control of the training/transfer stimuli.

Case Study 2: Michael

Brief Case History

Michael was six years, two months old when an NPA was accomplished. At the time of referral to our clinic he was considered to be approximately 25 to 50 percent intelligible by his parents and teachers. Michael was a late talker who used gestures to communicate until approximately two and one half years of age. His medical history was unremarkable. Hearing and functioning of the speech mechanism were normal. Reportedly, Mark had made excellent progress in speech services in the schools. The clinician had been working on both his language and his speech, using a fairly traditional sequence of sound stimulation and production activities. Michael was extremely easy to work with and motivated to work on his speech. He had been referred to a summer phonology clinic for the opportunity to have intensive work on his remaining errors.

NPA Analysis

NPA Data Sheets

The complete NPA data sheets are on pages 88 to 96. Additional interpretation and analyses follow on page 97.

Phonetic Analysis

As indicated in the NPA phonetic inventory, Michael had at least one correct instance of each of the 24 consonants, except for /ʒ/, /tʃ/ and /dʒ/ which were not glossed. As noted on the Summary Sheet, however, Michael's production of sibilants was characterized by prominent lip rounding. Tongue position for sibilants was posterior in the oral cavity, with some productions sounding almost lateralized. This curious posture of the tongue and lips was distracting cosmetically, and could contribute to Michael's lowered intelligibility.

In addition to the distortions of sibilants, Michael had a variety of sound changes on vowels and diphthongs; for example, [hɪk/hʊk], [beɪs/bɔɪz], [beɪg/bɪg],[mʌpd/mæpd]. Certain lexical items were consistently associated with vowel substitutions and distortions; other items, however, were inconsistent. Most of his vowel substitutions contained neutralized or lowered vowels, but he also replaced back vowels with front vowels.

These phonetic data are important to incorporate in an overall view of Michael's phonology and his management needs. He does have in his phonetic inventory, all of the consonant and vowel sounds. His context-free distortions of both consonants and vowels, however, is puzzling. Possibly, these distortions could be residuals from response development cues used in the speech management he had received (see Shriberg, in press, for a behavioral analysis of such data). They also might reflect his late onset of speech, followed by a period of rapid development of the phonetic inventory. His distortion and substitution errors could have been the product of his attempting to "put something in" rather than simplifying by deletion, a process seldom used. Posterior tongue position and lip rounding for sibilants could be related to vowel errors, as some generalized gradient of lip rounding for back vowels.

Speculations aside, Michael's vowel errors and peculiar form of sibilant distortions are reducing intelligibility, because his consonant system itself is not that severely involved. These issues will be addressed in a later discussion of management approaches.

Process Analysis

On the basis of the coded data, Michael's phonological sound changes are essentially limited to three processes: (1) Final Consonant Deletion, (2) Liquid Simplification, and (3) Cluster Reduction.

1. Final Consonant Deletion

Michael sometimes deletes /n/, /t/, /d/, and /l/ in word-final position. These data are curious as they span several stages of Renfrew's observed 10 stages of dissolution of this

Child Michael DOB _____ Age 6-2
Sampling Date _____ Analysis Date _____
Clinician _____

NPA TRANSCRIPTION SHEET
Shriberg and Kwiatkowski
John Wiley & Sons Copyright 1980 NPA

Comments on Sample Conditions _____

Item No.	GLOSS	TRANSCRIPTION	Item No.	GLOSS	TRANSCRIPTION
1	I can go water skiing	aɪ kæ go watɚ (skiŋ)	11	I can hardly	aɪ kn̩ haɪi
2	I can go camping	aɪ kæ go kæmpɪŋ	12	like when some-body ride my bike in (the) lake	laɪk wen sʌmbɑdɪ waɪd maɪ baɪk ɔn maɪ leɪk
3	swimming	swimiŋ	13	my old bike	maɪ ol baɪk
4	ride bikes down to the park	waɪ baɪks daʊ tu da park	14	we went to a boat landing	wi went tu ə bot lændɪŋ
5	when we been camping we ride bikes all day	wen wi ben kæmpɪŋ wi waɪd baɪks aʊ deɪ	15	and then some-body ride my bike right in the water	æn ʔɛn sʌmbɑdi waɪ maɪ baɪk waɪt ɪn na wadɚ
6	all day	aʊ deɪ	16	and then – said them can't find it	æn den sed dem kænt faɪn ɪt
7	we went round the block	wi wen waʊnd da blak	17	(them) never could	den nevɚ kʊd
8	we (had) big puddles down there you know	wi wʌ bɪg pʌdəz daʊn ðeɪʏ ja no	18	we got it out – now	wi gat ɪt aʊt naʊ
9	and where we went and me and my friend I took and went	æn wer wi went ted n̩ mi maɪ frend aɪ tʌk n̩ went	19	it's in the garage	ɪt ɪn da gawadʒ
10	in the puddle	ɪn da pʌdə	20	there got a flat tire	der gat ə faʊ taɪʏ

NPA TRANSCRIPTION SHEET

Shriberg and Kwiatkowski
John Wiley & Sons   Copyright 1980 NPA

Child _Michael_   DOB _____   Age _6-2_
Sampling _____   Analysis _____
Date _____   Date _____
Clinician _____

Comments on _____
Sample _____
Conditions _____

Item No.	GLOSS	TRANSCRIPTION	Item No.	GLOSS	TRANSCRIPTION
21	we ain't gonna buy a new tire	wi eint gana bai ə nu tai (ə)	31	I forgot its) name	ʌ fəgat it neim
22	I got a different bike	ai gat ə difwent baik	32	I think it up in	ai θiŋk it ʌp in
23	I buy it with my own money	ai bai it wif mai on mani	33	I been up there once	ai bin ʌp dɜ wʌns
24	in my bank	in ma beiŋk	34	some - (lake) (snake)	sʌm let sneik
25	I took it out	ai tuk it aut	35	there's river	dʌz wivɜ
26	I have it in my bank	ai hæv it in mai beiŋk	36	we went some- where are real big snake	wi wen sʌmwɜ a wil big raks
27	what no that rumble-bee that stinging me	wʌt no dæ bəmbəl bi dæt stiŋiŋ mi	37	I can't climb em, but	ai kæ kaim əm bʌ
28	yeah see	jæ si	38	we went right up there like this - I been ready	wi went wait wen ʌp dɜ lai dis ai bin wedi
29	and its stinging me	æn its stiŋiŋ mi	39	to climb em ... it's raining	tu kaim əm bʌt dɜs star weni
30	my mommy buried it, when her come home from up in somewhere camping	mai mami baid it wen eh kʌm hom fʌm ʌp in sʌmwɜ kæmpiŋ	40	out so I can't climb them	aut so ai kæn kaim em

NPA TRANSCRIPTION SHEET

Shriberg and Kwiatkowski
John Wiley & Sons   Copyright 1980 NPA

Child __Michael__   DOB _____   Age __6-2__
Sampling Date _____   Analysis Date _____
Clinician _____

Comments on
Sample
Conditions

Item No.	GLOSS	TRANSCRIPTION
41	yeah that what my dad said	jæ dæt wʌt maɪ dæd sɛ
→ 42	oh, I (remember) name, yeah	O aɪ (wɛn baɪ) neɪm jæ
43	Mississippi	mɪsɪsɪpi
44	did you ever go up there	dɪ ju ɛdɛ goʊ ʌp dɛr
45	my mommy fell down the waterfall	maɪ mami fɛ daʊn da watɔfɔl
46	a pier got broke down	a pɪr gat bok daʊn
47	and there was a waterfall right by her	æn dɛ wʌz ə wadəfal waɪ baɪ hɚ
48	and she went right down it	æn ʃi wɛnt waɪt daʊn ɪt
49	or her was or nothing	no zɛm rɪɥ oʊ naɪɥʊ
50	but somebody got her out	bʌt sʌmbɛdi gat ə aʊt

Item No.	GLOSS	TRANSCRIPTION
51	try my mommy's purse	baɪ maɪ mamiz pʊs
52	my mommy	maɪ mami
53	somebody put it down and pull it right up	sʌmbadi pʊt ɪt daʊn æn pʊl ɪt waɪt ʌp

NPA CODING SHEET

Shriberg and Kwiatkowski
John Wiley & Sons   Copyright 1980 NPA

Child: **Michael** DOB: _____ Age: **6-2**
Sampling _____ Analysis _____
Date _____ Date _____
Clinician _____

Coding Sheet: [A] Nasals; Glides; Liquids
Page No. **1**
Total Words Entered **40**
Sounds: [m, n, ŋ, w, j, l, r]

Column headings: 1 CV · 2 VC · 3 CVC · 4 C^n V(C) · 5 (C)VC^n · 6 Two-Syllable · 7 Three+ Syllable (each with Gloss / Trans. / Code)

Sound	Category	#	Gloss	Trans.	Code
m	CV		my	mi	C
m	CV	9	my	MAI	C
m	CVC	14	them	dɛm	S C
m	CVC	30	come	kʌm	C
m	CVC	30	home	hom	C
m	CVC	31	name	neim	C
m	Two-Syllable	33	money	mʌni	C
m	Two-Syllable	45	mommy	mami	C
m	Two-Syllable	51	mommy's	mamiz	C
m	Three+ Syllable	43	Mississippi	misisipi	C
n	CV	8	know	no	C
n	CV	18	now	naʊ	C
n	CV	21	new	nu	C
n	CV	27	no	no	C
n	VC	10	in	ɪn	C
n	VC	23	own	on	C
n	CVC	1	can	kæ	C FCD
n	CVC	4	down	daʊ	C FCD
n	CVC	5	when	wɛn	C
n	CVC	5	been	bɛn	C
n	CVC	15	then	tɛn	C
n	Two-Syllable	17	never	nɛvɚ	C
n	Two-Syllable	49	nothing	nʌθɪŋ	C
ŋ	CVC				C
w	CV	5	one	wɪ	C
w	CVC	47	will	wɪl	S C
w	Two-Syllable	1	water	watɚ	C
w	Two-Syllable	14	landing	lændɪŋ	C
w	Three+ Syllable	45	waterfall	watɚfɔl	C
j	CV	8	you	ja	C
j	CV	28	yeah	jæ	C
l	VC		all	ɔl	FCD
l	CVC	36	real	wil	S C
l	CVC	45	fell	fɛ	C IFCD
l	CVC	53	pull	pʊl	C
r	CVC	8	share	fɛir	C
r	CVC	9	there	wɛr	C
r	CVC	46	pier	pir	C
r	CVC	20	tire	taɪr	C
r	Two-Syllable	35	river	wivɚ	C
r	Two-Syllable	38	ready	wɛdi	C
r	Two-Syllable	39	mining	wɛni	C

NPA CODING SHEET

Shriberg and Kwiatkowski
John Wiley & Sons   Copyright 1980 NPA

Child __Michael__   DOB __6-2__
Age ____
Sampling ____   Analysis ____
Date ____   Date ____
Clinician ____

Total Words Entered ____
Sounds: [m, n, ŋ, w, j, l, r]

Sound	1 CV Gloss	Trans.	Code	2 VC Gloss	Trans.	Code	3 CVC Gloss	Trans.	Code	4 C^n V(C) Gloss	Trans.	Code	5 (C)VC^n Gloss	Trans.	Code	6 Two-Syllable Gloss	Trans.	Code	7 Three⁺ Syllable Gloss	Trans.	Code
m							34 home	sʌm	C I C												
n																					
ŋ																					
w																					
j																					
l																					
r																					

NPA CODING SHEET

Shriberg and Kwiatkowski
John Wiley & Sons   Copyright 1980 NPA

Child: **Michael**   DOB **6-2**   Age _____
Sampling Date _____   Analysis Date _____
Clinician _____

Coding Sheet: **B** Stops
Page No. **1**
Total Words Entered **44**
Sounds: [p, b, t, d, k, g,]

Sound	1 CV (Gloss / Trans. / Code)	2 VC (Gloss / Trans. / Code)	3 CVC (Gloss / Trans. / Code)	4 Cⁿ V(C) (Gloss / Trans. / Code)	5 (C)VCⁿ (Gloss / Trans. / Code)	6 Two-Syllable (Gloss / Trans. / Code)	7 Three⁺ Syllable (Gloss / Trans. / Code)
p		30 up / ʌp / C				8 spindler / pɪdəz / C ; 10 spindler / epʌd / C	
b	21 hey / baɪ / C ; 47 by / baɪ / C			7 blink / blak / C|C ; 46 broke / bok / CR|C			27 rumble... / bʌmbɔlbi / C
t	4 to / tu / C	16 it / ɪt / C ; 18 out / art / C	14 bought / bot / C|C ; 15 right / wait / LS|C ; 18 got / gat / C|C ; 27 what / wʌt / C|C ; 27 that / dæ / S|FcD ; 37 out / bʌ / C|FcD ; 59 put / pʌt / C|C		7 went / wɛn / C|CR ; 16 can't / kænt / C|C ; 39 start / star / C|CR		
d	5 day / deɪ / C		4 ride / waɪ / ST|FcD ; 9 Ted / ted / C|C ; 16 said / sɛd / C|C ; 17 could / kʌd / C ; 30 jumped / baɪd / C|C		7 round / warnd / LS|C ; 9 friend / frɛnd / C|C ; 13 old / ol / CR ; 16 find / faɪn / C|CR	23 different / difwɛnt / C	
k			9 took / tʌk / C|C ; 12 like / laɪk / C|C ; 13 bike / baɪk / C|C ; 12 lake / leɪk / C|C	37 clint / kaɪm / CR|C	4 park / park / C|C ; 24 frank / beɪŋk / C|C ; 32 think / θɪŋk / C|C	2 camping / kæmpɪŋ / C	
g	1 go / go / C		8 dig / big / C|C			18 garage / gawadʒ / C	

Child __Michael__ DOB _____ Age __6-2__
Sampling _____ Analysis _____
Date _____ Date _____
Clinician _____

NPA CODING SHEET

Shriberg and Kwiatkowski   Copyright 1980 NPA
John Wiley & Sons

Coding Sheet: ☐B Stops
Page No. __2__

Total Words Entered _____
Sounds: [p, b, t, d, k, g,]

Sound	1 CV Gloss	Trans.	Code	2 VC Gloss	Trans.	Code	3 CVC Gloss	Trans.	Code	4 Cⁿ V(C) Gloss	Trans.	Code	5 (C) VCⁿ Gloss	Trans.	Code	6 Two-Syllable Gloss	Trans.	Code	7 Three⁺ Syllable Gloss	Trans.	Code
p																					
b																					
t																					
d							"dad	dæd	CIC												
							"did	dɪ	CIFCD												
k																					
g																					

NPA CODING SHEET

Shriberg and Kwiatkowski
John Wiley & Sons   Copyright 1980 NPA

Child: Michael   DOB ___ Age **6-2**
Sampling ___ Analysis ___
Date ___ Date ___
Clinician ___

Coding Sheet: [C] Fricatives; Affricates
Page No. **1**
Total Words Entered **22**
Sounds: [h, f, v, θ, ð, s, z, ʃ, ʒ, tʃ, dʒ]

Sound	1 CV Gloss	Trans.	Code	2 VC Gloss	Trans.	Code	3 CVC Gloss	Trans.	Code	4 Cⁿ V(C) Gloss	Trans.	Code	5 (C)VCⁿ Gloss	Trans.	Code	6 Two-Syllable Gloss	Trans.	Code	7 Three⁺ Syllable Gloss	Trans.	Code
h																¹¹hardly	hʌji	C			
f							²⁶have	hæv	C	²⁰flat	fæʊ	CR				³¹forgot	fəgɑt	C			
										³⁰from	fʌm	CRC									
v							²³with	wɪf	C							⁴⁴ever	ɛdɛ	C			
θ																					
ð	⁴the	də	S																		
s	²⁸see	sɪ	C				³⁸this	dɪs	S C				⁴likes	baɪks	C C	³swimming	swɪmɪŋ	C	¹²somebody	sʌmbʌdi	C
							⁵¹purse	pʊs	C C				⁹it(s)	ɪt	CR	²⁷stinging	stɪŋɪŋ	C			
													³³once	wʌns	C C	³⁰somewhere	sʌmwɔ˞	C			
													³⁶rocks	rɑks	C C						
z							⁴⁷was	wʌz	C				³⁵there's	dɑz	CR						
ʃ	⁴⁸she	ʃi	C																		
ʒ																					
tʃ																					
dʒ																					

NPA SUMMARY SHEET

Shriberg and Kwiatkowski
John Wiley & Sons   Copyright 1980 NPA

Child __Michael__   DOB __6-2__ Age _____
Sampling Date _____   Analysis Date _____
Clinician _____

Total Words Entered (A + B + C) __109__

Phonetic Inventory

	m	n	ŋ	w	j	p	b	t	d	k	g	h	f	v	θ	ð	s	z	ʃ	ʒ	tʃ	dʒ	l	r
Correct Anywhere →	x	x	x	x	x	x	x	x	x	x	x	x	x	x	x		x	x	x		x	x	x	x
Appears Anywhere →																								
Glossed Never Correct; Never Appears →																								
Never Glossed; Never Appears →																x				x				

1 — Final Consonant Deletion

m	n	ŋ	w	j	p	b	t	d	k	g	h	f	v	θ	ð	s	z	ʃ	ʒ	tʃ	dʒ	l	r
O	⊘	-			-	⊘	⊘	⊘	O	O		-	O	O	-	O	O	-	-	-	-	⊘	O

2 — Velar Fronting

Initial →	O
Final →	O

3 — Stopping

	h	f	v	θ	ð	s	z	ʃ	ʒ	tʃ	dʒ
Initial →	O	O	-	O	⊘	O	O	-	-	-	-
Final →	-	-	O	O	-	O	O	-	-	-	-

4 — Palatal Fronting

	ʃ	ʒ	tʃ	dʒ
Initial →	O	-	-	-
Final →	-	-	-	-

5 — Liquid Simplification

	l	r
	✓	O
	O	O

6

Progressive Assimilations	Regressive Assimilations
none	none

7 — Cluster Reduction

	Correct	Reduced
Initial Clusters →	bl fr st	F/Fl F/Fr K/Kl b/br
Final Clusters →	nt rk nd ŋk <u>Ks</u> <u>ns</u>	<u>z/rz</u> r/rt n/nt l/ld <u>t/ts</u> n/nd

8 — Unstressed Syllable Deletion

	Two Syllable	Three+ Syllable
n	21	4
Deletions n	0	0
% Deletions	0	0

Notes: __see Additional Analysis__

process (see Appendix A). Of possible relevance is the fact that each of the sounds Michael deletes in the final position is an alveolar. Interestingly, he does not delete /k/ or /g/, sounds that according to Renfrew's stage data, are usually among the last to be correct in final position. Recall that Michael uses a retracted tongue position for sibilants; dorsovelar contact, of course, is also required for /k/ and /g/. His infrequent use of Final Consonant Deletion in CVC words (22 percent), in any case, indicates that this process is resolving.

2. Liquid Simplification

Michael's errors on liquids are limited to [w/r] on occasion, in the initial position, placing him in Stage 2 of Liquid Simplification. His demonstrated ability to produce acceptable [ɝ] and [ɚ] suggests that this process too, should eventually resolve without intervention. Again, some curious phonetic facts: Michael produces the rhotacized vowels [ɝ] and [ɚ] correctly, while erring on assumedly less difficult vowels.

3. Cluster Reduction

Michael's reductions of clusters place him at Stage 2 of the four stages described b Ingram, with deletions of both the marked and the unmarked members of the cluster. / commonly observed in NPA analyses, clusters are likely candidates for context-functi analyses, as we describe next.

Context-Function Analysis

Of the data available on the Transcription Sheets, two context-function analyses re possible: analysis of the inconsistent Final Consonant Deletions and analysis of clus rs.

Because Final Consonant Deletion occurs so infrequently, worksheet analy s is not warranted. Upon inspection, the data on the Transcription Sheets do not sugg t an underlying pattern within the four words in which the final consonant is dele d or correct at least once.*

Variability in final cluster productions presents an opportunity to explore whether context-function variables are associated with this process. Specifically, the grammatical function of /t/ and /d/ as past tense morphemes could be of interest because Michael does have a delay in language production and because he sometimes deleted these sounds when they occurred as singletons in the final position.

Using a modification of the worksheet format suggested in the Guidelines (because Michael's utterances often contained *several* target words), we listed in Tables 5 and 6 the most interesting entries from the Transcription Sheets. Scanning the column data, we cannot perceive a pattern to Michael's correct versus reduced clusters. Possibly, he is more often correct when the following word begins with /t/ or /d/.† Perhaps if these data were reviewed from the original tape recording, we might find that some other variable (for example, stress) is associated differentially with cluster production.

The context-function analysis as presented here is included only as an example of one type of worksheet procedure. In practice, the clinician becomes able to perceive whether processes may be associated with structure-function variables just by observing a few key pieces of data. Such analyses are basic to the integrated approach to language-speech services discussed throughout this text. Case Study No. 4 is included in this text to illustrate in detail, the types of inquiry procedures that are needed and that may someday become clinically routine.

---

* Inspect these words yourself on the Transcription Sheets: "down," "that," "but," and "ride." Do you perceive any common context or function factor in the sentences in which the final consonants in each of these words are variably deleted?

† Notice that such data could reflect segmentation problems in transcribing continuous speech.

Table 5 Some entries from Michael's transcription sheets

Sheet/Item Number	Glossed Item	Transcription	Correct	Incorrect
1-5	we <u>went</u> <u>round</u> the block	[wi wɛ̃n waʊ̃nd də blak]	②	①
1-7	and where we <u>went</u> Ted and me my <u>friend</u> I took — and <u>went</u>	[ən wɛr wi wɛ̃nt tɛd n̩ mi maɪ frɛ̃nd aɪ tʊk — n̩ wɛ̃nt]	③④⑤	
1-12	we <u>went</u> to a boat landing	[wi wɛ̃nt tu ə bot /ændɪŋ]	⑥	
1-13	and then—said them <u>can't</u> <u>find</u> it	[æn dɛn—sɛd dɛm kæ̃nt faɪn ɪt]	⑦	⑧
2-11	we went somewhere — are real big rocks	[wi wɛ̃n sʌmwɛr— a wil bɪg raks]		⑨
2-12	I <u>can't</u> climb them but	[aɪ kæ̃ kaɪm əm bʌ]		⑩
2-13	we <u>went</u> right <u>went</u> up there...	[wi wɛ̃nt waɪt wɛ̃n ʌp dɛr]	⑪	⑫
2-15	out so I <u>can't</u> climb them	[aʊt so aɪ kæ̃n kaɪm ɛm]		⑬
3-3	and she <u>went</u> right down it	[ən ʃi wɛ̃nt waɪt daʊn ɪt]	⑭	

Implications of NPA Data for Management Programming

Michael's rapid gains in both speech and language production are expected to continue. A management program should focus on two areas: (1) self-monitoring of vowel substitutions, and (2) elimination of lip rounding and tongue bunching (bunching the tongue like a fist in the back of the mouth).

1. Self-Monitoring of Vowel Substitutions

Because vowel substitutions are reducing Michael's intelligibility, some portion of the management program should be directed toward reducing or eliminating them. Michael can articulate all vowels correctly, but he does not always do so—even in simple canonical forms. Procedures that ask him to self-monitor and reinforce himself for self-correction seem warranted. That is, the problem requires an identification program, not an articulation program. As Michael talks in words, phrases, sentences, and continuous speech, he learns to identify and self-correct immediately, all vowel substitutions.

Table 6 A modified worksheet for analysis of final clusters

Worksheet: Final Clusters /nt/ , /nd/

	Context Variables			Function Variables		
	Following Word Begins With:			Verb Form	Morpheme Final	Contraction
	a vowel	a /t/ or a /d/	an /r/ or a /w/			
Correct Clusters						
② (reduced from /d/)		X			X	
③		X				
④	X				X	
⑤			X	X	X	
⑥		X		X	X	
⑦						X
⑪			X	X	X	
⑭			X	X	X	
Incorrect Clusters						
①			X	X	X	
⑧	X			X	X	
⑨				X		
⑩						X
⑫	X			X	X	
⑬						X

2. Eliminate Lip Rounding and Tongue Bunching

The origin of Michael's lip rounding and tongue bunching behaviors on sibilants is interesting to speculate about, but beyond reclaim. As suggested earlier, he may have acquired these behaviors himself in his own efforts to use those speech sounds rapidly piling up in his phonetic inventory, or he may have developed these responses somewhere in the course of management. Or possibly, his lip rounding behaviors on sibilants are associated in some way with his vowel errors, Whichever their origin, these articulatory gestures require attention. The suggestion would be for a discrimination program in which he learns to discriminate lip rounding from non-lip rounding in gradually more complex linguistic environments. Correlated with these efforts would be a response development program for /s/ that stressed more anterior tongue posture, proper tongue shape, and central air emission.

Summary

These data indicate that Michael's speech is essentially *free* of the eight phonological processes affecting consonants—which is why this case study was included. Attention to the two management objectives above with primary work on language elements would seem to be the most productive approach. The Transcription Sheets provide ample illustrations of his delays in acquisition of grammatical morphemes. With these NPA data consolidated as illustrated here, the clinician should be able to proceed with an integrated *language* production program—a program that includes attention to Michael's remaining needs in speech development.

Case Study 3: Toby

Brief Case History

When Toby was first evaluated at five years by his school speech-language pathologist he was described by his mother as "a late talker just like his older brother." Toby did not use two-word utterances until he was approximately three years old. His older brother experienced rapid improvement in speech acquisition between five and six years. Toby's mother viewed Toby as more severely delayed than his brother. She estimated Toby's intelligibility at approximately 25 percent. Medical and psychosocial history were unremarkable; Toby's hearing and oral mechanism were normal in structure and function. A comprehensive cognitive and language assessment indicated that his cognitive and comprehension development were within normal limits, but that his productive language was approximately one year delayed. At the time of the following NPA analysis, Toby had received only minimal speech management.

NPA Analysis

NPA Data Sheets

This case example is included to illustrate the use of narrow phonetic transcription in an NPA analysis. As discussed in the text, narrow phonetic transcription is useful, but necessary only for some purposes. This example retains all the diacritics used in the original case materials, in order to illustrate use of some of the diacritics listed on page 63.

The completed NPA data sheets are on pages 102 through 110. Additional interpretation and analyses follow on page 111.

Phonetic Analysis

Inspection of the Transcription Sheets and the Summary Sheet indicates that Toby was producing at least one sound within all six manner classes. Among those sounds not correct:

/ʒ/ was never glossed.

/ʃ/ was usually replaced by [tʃ].

/j/ was deleted (one token).

/θ/ and /ð/ were deleted or replaced by [f] or a frictionalized /t/, [ṱ].

/g/ and /z/ were usually deleted or replaced; however, voiceless cognates of each sound, [k] and [s], occurred at least once in the sample.

These data illustrate nicely the difference between phonetic mastery, in the sense of demonstrated ability to say a sound correctly—and phonological competence. Toby's severe intelligibility deficit can not be traced to a reduced inventory of speech sounds, for he can articulate 79 percent (19 out of 24) of the consonants correctly and he can articulate all vowels and diphthongs correctly. Moreover, many of his speech sound changes are not within the eight "natural" processes coded in the NPA procedures. Among these uncodable (Type 3b) sound changes are

1. Extensive deletions of initial consonants, including glides, /w/, /j/, liquids /l/, /r/, and the fricative /h/.

2. Use of a glottal stop to replace both initial and final consonants (although some phonologists view some forms of glottalization as "natural").

3. Use of [tʃ] to replace both some fricatives, /s/, /ʃ/ and some stops, /t/, /k/.

4. Substitution of [b/m] (observed only once in the sample, but confirmed in additional samples).

5. Some substitutions of [k] for /t/ in final position, for example, [ik] for "eat."

These sound changes are interesting because they do not follow from any simple metric of "ease of articulation." For example, the liquids /l/ and /r/ generally are preserved, whereas the glides /w/ and /j/ and the fricative /h/ are not. Furthermore, these data do not form a coherent picture that could implicate a structural or functional problem with the speech mechanism, as suggested, for example, in an earlier case example (see Jack, page 67). Toby's rate of utterance, pitch, loudness, and duration characteristics are normal; neither voicing problems (laryngeal) nor context-free hypernasality (velopharyngeal) are evident. Rather, Toby's extensive use of deletion is viewed as a phonological process that simplifies all surface forms in order to permit talking. Even simple CV and VC forms are sometimes reduced to a vowel—a behavior that suggests that this simplification process operates across place-manner features of sounds and across canonical forms.

Process Analysis

On many sounds, Toby's extensive use of initial and final consonant deletion obviates the operation of other processes.* Notice that of the 15 final consonants for which data are available he "sometimes" or "always" deletes 11 (73 percent) of these. Because the NPA procedure does not allow for multiple processes to apply to a target sound, deleted sounds can not be coded for any other process. Toby's array of sound changes is both interesting of itself and instructive, in terms of NPA methodology. For these reasons, brief comment will be made on each of the eight processes, including comments on methodological issues.

---

* Recall that the symbol "O" as used on the Summary Sheet means that a process does not occur for a sound. It does not necessarily mean that the sound is always produced correctly, however, because another process earlier in the coding sequence (for example, FCD) could account for the sound change.

NPA TRANSCRIPTION SHEET

Shriberg and Kwiatkowski Copyright 1980 NPA
John Wiley & Sons

Child __Toby__   DOB _____ Age __5-8__
Sampling Date _____ Analysis _____
Date _____
Clinician _____

Comments on _____
Sample _____
Conditions _____

Item No.	GLOSS	TRANSCRIPTION
1	putting on his pants and shirt	pᶻɪ ɒn ɪ pᶻã̃ ɪ tʃɝ②
2	going to bed	doĩ tu bɛ̰
3	get up and wash his face	dɛ̰ ˅ʌp ̃ɛ ə̃ ⓦ fɛɪ:
4	brush his teeth	bʌ ɪ tʰiː②
5	and comb his hair	æn tʃʊɹm ɪ ʔʌr:
6	and eat	̃ɛ iːkʰ
7	and all the (his) stuff what gonna eat	æ ɔ æ dʌv wʌt i do iːk
8	egg	ɛɪ:
9	bacon	bɛɪʔã̃
10	butter	bʌbɚ

Item No.	GLOSS	TRANSCRIPTION
11	orange juice	̃ʌ tʃʊ̃
12	toast	tʃʊɹə
13	milk and water	bɔkʰ ̃ɛ ãɹɚ
14	two and three (reading a book)	tu ̃ɛ fɪ ⓘ̃ə bʊkʰ
15	he(s) going to bed and his dog	hi dɔɪŋ tu bɛ ̃ɛ i dɔ:
16	and his dog came in his bed	̃ɛ hɪ dɔ kɛɪ ɪ hɪ bɛ
17	and he got up	̃ɛ ̃ɪ dã ⓤ̰
18	and he(s) pulling his cover	̃ɛn hi pʊ̃ɪ̃ŋ ɪ̰ tʃʌvɚ
19	and dog sleeping and he ain't	̃ɛ dɔ ipĩŋ ̃ɛ ɪ ɛ̃ɪ
20	he taking bath	iː teʔɪn baː

Child __Toby__
DOB _____ Age __5-8__
Sampling _____ Analysis _____
Date _____ Date _____
Clinician _____

NPA TRANSCRIPTION SHEET
Shriberg and Kwiatkowski   Copyright 1980 NPA
John Wiley & Sons

Comments on _____
Sample _____
Conditions _____

Item No.	GLOSS	TRANSCRIPTION	Item No.	GLOSS	TRANSCRIPTION
21	(wiping) himself off	xx ɪtʃɛʳf ɔf	31	like that	aɪʔ æe̞
22	dog got water off	dɔg dḁʔ ɔwə ɔf	32	but that is brown	bʌ a ɪ brã:ᵛ
23	shakin	ʃeɪʔɛ̃	33	blue	blu
24	put his tee shirt on	pᵕɪ i t̬ɪtʃɚⓣ an	34	tie his shoe	t̃aɪ ɪ̞ ʧu
25	put his coat on	pᵕəⓣ i ʧokᵛ ã̩n	35	one sock on	õ t̬s̪ak õ
26	put his pants (on)	pə ɪ pã̃ɪ: jã	36	shoe	ʧuᵊ
27	zip um	dʒɪp ʌm	37	brush his teeth	baᵛ i t̬ɪf̠
28	zipper	dʒɪpə̞	38	toothpaste	ʧupeɪ
29	buckle his belt	bʌʔ i bɔkʰ	39	that all going on the floor	ʔɔ ɔ dõ̃ɪ ã̃ ɪ fɔᵛ
30	buckle his belt	bʌʔᵒ e (bɔk)	40	comb his hair	ʧʌm ɪ̞ ɝ

NPA TRANSCRIPTION SHEET

Shriberg and Kwiatkowski
John Wiley & Sons   Copyright 1980 NPA

Child **Toby**   DOB ___   Age **5-8**
Sampling ___   Analysis ___
Date ___   Date ___
Clinician ___

Comments on ___
Sample ___
Conditions ___

Item No.	GLOSS	TRANSCRIPTION	Item No.	GLOSS	TRANSCRIPTION
41	rid	æ:	51	spill	p=ʊ
42	cutting (out) (people)	tʃʌĩ xxx	52	paint	p=ẽɪ
43	cutting out little people	tʃʌĩ ɔ wɛʳ piʔʃ	53	water	ʋɛm:c
44	and her pasting	æ̃ ɝ peɪˣ	54	he carrying a dog	hi tʃærɪɪŋ ə bɔg
45	coloring that	tʃʌrɪŋ ɛ	55	he setting it down	hi tʃeʔĩ ɪ daːʳ
46	and her sleeping	ɛ ɝ ipĩ	56	her carrying a dog	ɝ taɹɪŋ ə bɔg
47	and he going	ɛ̃ i doĩ	57	her jump over and frog watch	dʒʌmp ɔʋəʳ ɝ / a ẽ fa wak
48	in hallway	ɪ ɔwɛɪ	58	frog and girl watch	fɑc ẽ dʒɝl aːk
49	painting	p=ẽɪ ĩ	59	watch him	ʔɑ: ʔɪm
50	paint spill	p=ẽɪ p=ʊ	60	now her and frog watch her	nɑ: ɝ (ẽ) boʳ ẽ / fɔ æ̃ ɝ

NPA TRANSCRIPTION SHEET

Shriberg and Kwiatkowski
John Wiley & Sons Copyright 1980 NPA

Child __Toby__ DOB _____ Age __5-8__
Sampling _____ Analysis _____
Date _____ Date _____
Clinician _____

Page No. __4__

Comments on _____
Sample _____
Conditions _____

Item No.	GLOSS	TRANSCRIPTION	Item No.	GLOSS	TRANSCRIPTION
61	fall in, but he didn't	fɔːɹ ɪ̃ bʌʔ iː dɪ̃ʔ			
62	jump over	dʒʌmp oʊvə			
63	splash	p⁼æ̃ː			
64	and he chasing him	ɛ̃ i ʧeɪ̃ ɪ̃			
65	dog chasing bird	gɔ ʧeɪɪ bɝː			
66	and he got hurt	eɪ̃ daʔ ɝ			
67	you do	ʌp e			

NPA CODING SHEET

Shriberg and Kwiatkowski
John Wiley & Sons   Copyright 1980 NPA

Child __Toby__
Sampling ____   DOB __5-8__
Date ____   Age __5-8__
Clinician ____   Analysis ____
Date ____

Coding Sheet: [A] Nasals; Glides; Liquids
Page No. _1_
Total Words Entered _17_
Sounds: [m,n,ŋ,w,j,l,r]

Sound	1 CV			2 VC			3 CVC			4 Cⁿ V(C)				5 (C) VCⁿ				6 Two-Syllable			7 Three⁺ Syllable		
	Gloss	Trans.	Code	Gloss	Trans.	Code	Gloss	Trans.	Code	Gloss	Trans.	Code	Gloss	Trans.	Code	Gloss	Trans.	Code	Gloss	Trans.	Code	
m	⁶ more na:		²⁷ um	ʌm	C	⁵ comb	+ĵoum	C														
						¹⁶ came	Kɛɪ	C⎸FCD														
						⁵⁹ him	ʔɪm	C														
n			¹⁰ on	ɔn	C	³⁵ one	ə̃	⌀⎸FCD														
			¹⁶ in	ɪ	FCD	⁵⁵ down	da:ṽ	C⎸FCD														
ŋ																						
w																⁴³ water	aɚ̆ɚ	C				
j	⁶⁷ you	e	⌀																			
l			⁷ all	C	FCD	⁵⁷ girl	dʒəl	vp⎸C								⁴³ little	ʌⁱ	usd				
						⁶¹ fall	fɔ:ᵛ	C⎸FCD															
r							⁵ hair	ʔʌr	C								¹¹ orange	ĩ	usd				

NPA CODING SHEET

Shriberg and Kwiatkowski
John Wiley & Sons   Copyright 1980 NPA

Child: Toby
DOB ___ Age 5-8
Sampling Date ___ Analysis Date ___
Clinician ___

Coding Sheet: B Stops
Page No. 1
Total Words Entered 51
Sounds: [p,b,t,d,k,g,]

Sound	**1 CV** Gloss	Trans.	Code	**2 VC** Gloss	Trans.	Code	**3 CVC** Gloss	Trans.	Code	**4 Cⁿ V(C)** Gloss	Trans.	Code	**5 (C) VCⁿ** Gloss	Trans.	Code	**6 Two-Syllable** Gloss	Trans.	Code	**7 Three+ Syllable** Gloss	Trans.	Code
p				³ up	ʌp	C	²⁷ zip	dʒɪp	C				⁵¹ jump	dʒʌmp	C	¹ putting	pʰ⁼ɪ	USD			
																¹⁷ pulling	pʰuɪŋ	C			
																⁴⁴ pasting	peɪ	C			
b	⁴⁹ my boy	boʸ	C							⁴ brush	bʌ	CR				⁹ bacon	beɪʔə̃	C			
										³² brown	brɑ̃ːʸ	C FCD				¹⁰ butter	bʌbɚ	C			
										³³ blue	blu	C				²⁹ knuckle	bʌʔ	USD			
t	²to	tu	C	⁶ eat	iːkʰ	C	³ get	dɛ̰	VF FCD				¹² treat	tʃoʊᵊ	CR	²⁰ taking	teɪɪn	C			
	¹⁴ two	tu	C	¹³ out	ɔ	FCD	⁷ what	wʌt	C				¹⁹ ain't	êɪ̃	CR	²⁴ t-shirt	tɪtsᵣ(t)ᵪ	CR			
	³⁴ too	tɑɪ	C	⁵⁵ it	ɪ	FCD	¹⁷ get	dɑ̰	VF FCD				²⁹ felt	bɔkʰ	C CR	³⁸ tooth-paste	tʃʌpeɪ	C			
							²⁴ put	pʰ⁼ɪ	C FCD				⁵⁰ paint	pʰ⁼êɪ	C CR						
							²⁵ coat	tʃoʊᵏ	C												
							³¹ that	æ̰	∅ FCD												
							³² hit	bʌ	C FCD												
							⁶⁶ hurt	ɝ	∅ FCD												
d	¹⁷ do	du	C				² red	bɛ̰ː	C FCD				⁴¹ didn't	dɪ̃ʔ	USD	² going	doɪ̃	USD			
							⁴¹ red	æ̰ː	∅ FCD							⁷ gonna	do	USD			
							⁶⁵ bird	bɝː	C FCD												
k							¹⁴ tooth	bɔ̰kʰ	C				¹³ milk	bɔkʰ	CR	¹⁸ cover	tʃʌvɚ	C	⁴⁴ coloring	tʃʌrɪŋ	C
							³¹ like	ɑɪʔ	∅							⁴² cutting	tʃʌɪ̃	C	⁵⁴ carrying	tʃæ̃rɪŋ	C
							³⁵ work	tʃɑk	C												
g				⁸ egg	eɪː	FCD	¹⁵ dog	dɔː	C FCD												

NPA CODING SHEET

Shriberg and Kwiatkowski

John Wiley & Sons   Copyright 1980 NPA

Child _Tony_

DOB _____   Age _5-8_

Sampling _____   Analysis _____

Date _____   Date _____

Clinician _____

Total Words Entered _____

Sounds: | p, b, t, d, k, g, |

Sound	1 CV Gloss	Trans.	Code	2 VC Gloss	Trans.	Code	3 CVC Gloss	Trans.	Code	4 C^n V(C) Gloss	Trans.	Code	5 (C)VC^n Gloss	Trans.	Code	6 Two-Syllable Gloss	Trans.	Code	7 Three+ Syllable Gloss	Trans.	Code
p																48 painting	$p^=$eɪ ĩ	c			
																53 purple	pɪʔɭ	c			
b																					
t																					
d																					
k																					
g																					

NPA CODING SHEET

Shriberg and Kwiatkowski

John Wiley & Sons   Copyright 1980 NPA

Child __Toby__   DOB _____   Age __5-8__

Sampling _____   Analysis _____

Date _____   Date _____

Clinician _____

Coding Sheet: [C] Fricatives; Affricates

Page No. __1__

Total Words Entered __30__

Sounds: [h, f, v, θ, ð, s, z, ʃ, ʒ, tʃ, dʒ]

Sound	1 CV Gloss	Trans.	Code	2 VC Gloss	Trans.	Code	3 CVC Gloss	Trans.	Code	4 Cⁿ V(C) Gloss	Trans.	Code	5 (C) VCⁿ Gloss	Trans.	Code	6 Two-Syllable Gloss	Trans.	Code	7 Three⁺ Syllable Gloss	Trans.	Code
h	¹⁹he i ∅ / ⁴⁴he ɜ ∅															²¹ him-self itʃɛvf C / ⁴⁸ hallway ɔwɛɪ C					
f				²¹ ff ɔf C						³⁹ floor foʊ CR / ⁵¹ frog fa CR											
v																⁵⁷ over oʊvɚ C					
θ							²⁰ mouth bæ: C FCD / ³⁷ teeth tif C			¹⁴ three fi CR											
ð	⁷ the æ ∅																				
s							³ face fɛɪ: C FCD / ¹¹ juice tʃu			⁷ stuff dʌv C FCD / ⁵³ splash pæ: C FCD / ⁵¹ spill pʊ CR			¹ pants pã C CR / ⁵⁴ lost bɔk C CR								
z	³²is I		I				⁷ his I ∅ FCD / ¹⁵ he(a) hi C FCD														
ʃ	³⁴ chair tʃu						³ wash 3 ∅ FCD									²⁸ zipper dʒɪpɚ C					
ʒ																²³ shaking tʃɛɪʔɛ̃ C					
tʃ							⁵⁷ watch a ∅ FCD									⁶⁴ chasing tʃɛɪ̃ĩ C					
dʒ																					

NPA SUMMARY SHEET

Shriberg and Kwiatkowski   Copyright 1980 NPA
John Wiley & Sons

Child __Toby__   DOB _____   Age __5-8__
Sampling Date _____   Analysis Date _____
Clinician _____

Total Words Entered (A + B + C) __100__

Phonetic Inventory

	m	n	ŋ	w	j	p	b	t	d	k	g	h	f	v	θ	ð	s	z	ʃ	ʒ	tʃ	dʒ	l	r
Correct Anywhere →	x	x		x	x	x	x	x	x	x		x	x	x		x	x				x	x	x	x
Appears Anywhere →																								
Glossed Never Correct; Never Appears →					x						x				x	x	x	x	x					
Never Glossed; Never Appears →																				x				

1 — Final Consonant Deletion

	m	n	ŋ	w	j	p	b	t	d	k	g	h	f	v	θ	ð	s	z	ʃ	ʒ	tʃ	dʒ	l	r
Final Consonant Deletion →	∅	∅	–	–		O	–	∅	✓	O	✓		O	–	∅	–	✓	✓	✓	–	–	–	∅	O

2 — Velar Fronting

Initial →	O	✓
Final →	O	O

3 — Stopping

	f	v	θ	ð	s	z	ʃ	ʒ	tʃ	dʒ
Initial →	O	–	–	–	O	O	O	O	O	–
Final →	O	–	O	O	O	O	–	O	–	O

4 — Palatal Fronting

	ʃ	ʒ	tʃ	dʒ
Initial →	O	–	O	O
Final →	O	–	–	O

5 — Liquid Simplification

Initial	Final
O	O
O	O

6

Progressive Assimilations	Regressive Assimilations
none	none

7 — Cluster Reduction

	Correct	Reduced
Initial Clusters →	br bl	p⁼/sp b/br f/fl
		d/st f/fr
		p⁼/spl f/br
Final Clusters →	mp	∅/st ∅/nt k/lk
		∅/nts k/lt
		k/ks

8 — Unstressed Syllable Deletion

	Two Syllable	Three⁺ Syllable
Deletions	n 27	n 2
Deletions	n 7	n 0
% Deletions	% 25	% 0

Notes: ___ See additional analysis

1. Final Consonant Deletion

Toby's pattern of Final Consonant Deletions can not be captured by one of Renfrew's 10 stages. Each of the six manner classes contains sounds that are "sometimes" or "always" deleted in word-final position. Particularly interesting is his deletion "sometimes" of final /m/ and final /n/, because nasals assumedly stabilize before stops and fricatives (Renfrew's Stage 4). As described in the Phonetic Analysis, nasal errors are seen also in the initial position [bɔk] for "milk," a manner error that could implicate velopharyngeal timing. Other signs of possible velopharyngeal involvement—such as context-free hypernasality—are not apparent, however. Toby's deletions of final nasals, which presumedly are early appearing sounds, provide additional support for the view that his deletion strategy is pervasive.

It is instructive to illustrate here how Toby marks stop and nasal consonants that he deletes. The following data appear on the Coding Sheets.

/n/		/t/		/d/	
"brown"	[brã:ʊ]	"get"	[dɛ]	"bed"	[bɛ:]
"one"	[ɔ̃]	"but"	[bʌ]	"red"	[ræ:]
"down"	[dã:ʊ]	"hurt"	[ɝ]	"bird"	[bɝ:]

Nasalization of the vowel in words with final /n/ marks the deleted final nasal. This is a Type la sound change that shows that Toby has acquired the feature change on the vowel, but deletes the consonant that conditions it. Similarly, looking at the examples for words ending in /d/ versus the words ending in /t/, Toby's vowels preceding the voiced stops /d/ are longer ([:]) than vowels preceding the voiceless final stop, /t/. Again, each of these context-sensitive sound changes, assimilative nasality, and vowel lengthening before voiced final obstruents, indicates that Toby is using the feature change rules (allophones) of adult phonology. Hence, although his surface forms are extensively simplified by deletion, these same forms also contain evidence that deletions occurred later in the derivation. Although the formal procedure for coding NPA data does not allow for ordered rules (with the exception of the assimilation/deletion sequence described for page 41), additional analysis procedures certainly can consider such possibilities. Using a modified rule notation, Toby's rules would be ordered as follows.

1. $V \rightarrow \tilde{V} /$ ___ C_{nas} # (vowels are nasalized before final nasal consonants).
2. $C_{nas} \rightarrow \emptyset /$ ___ # (final nasal consonants are deleted).

We have no difficulty accepting the utility of such ordered rules to "explain" data such as Toby's feature changes on vowels before word-final consonants. Indeed, we agree with phonologists who would view rules such as these as well motivated. Our goal in these NPA procedures, however, is to distinguish between the formal Summary, which generates reliable data from a series of formalized procedures, and the additional procedures which involve normative data and linguistic inquiry procedures. The former is accomplished in Coding and is summarized on the NPA Summary Sheet; the latter is available in the data for each NPA user to pursue, depending on his or her theoretical views of what constitutes a proper and useful phonological analysis.

To return to Toby's data, his use of deletion is easily the most prominent of his simplification processes. Notice that he simplifies even VC words ([ɪ] for "in," [ɔ] for "all," [ɪ] for "it"). Although his pattern of FCD defies classification by Renfrew's stage data, his behavior on prefinal consonant vowels suggests that he is "on the verge" of rapid improvement in final consonants. Later, we look more closely at how these data were used for management programming.

2. Velar Fronting

Because FCD usually operates on final /k/ and /g/, VF occurs sometimes only when these sound are in word-initial position. Toby is in the second of the two stages of Velar Fronting (see Appendix A) although his inconsistency is again, puzzling.

3. Stopping

As indicated on the Summary Sheet, Toby does not use Stopping as a simplification process. According to the entries in Appendix A, Toby could be considered at Stage 3 of the five stages of fricative production. But these data provide another important example of the need to thoroughly understand NPA procedures. Toby does not use Stopping on /s/ and /z/ assumedly because a deletion process usually operates first. From a research viewpoint it would be interesting to track just when Toby might begin to actually say stops for fricatives as his speech develops. That is, at what point in the development of his fricatives and the dissolution of FCD as a simplification strategy, might he begin to stop fricatives in certain canonical structures.

In any event, Toby's present data indicate that like other consonants, fricatives in both initial and final position in the word undergo deletion.

4. Palatal Fronting

Our definition of Palatal Fronting requires that one of four sounds /ʃ/, /ʒ/, /tʃ/, /dʒ/, be replaced by a more anterior sound. Toby often replaces one of these four sounds with another sound in this group (for example, [tʃu] for "shoe") or deletes the sound; however, he does not replace palatals with more anterior sounds. Notice that two important methodological operations are important in issues like this. First, some phoneticians would disagree with a decision to group all four sounds as palatals. If the affricates /tʃ/ and /dʒ/ are alternatively viewed as *alveolo*palatals, for example, then replacing /ʃ/ with /tʃ/ would satisfy the criterion of *fronting* a palatal. Our decision, however, is to group all four sounds as palatals, hence a substitution of this sort does not meet a "fronting" requirement. In other systems of phonological analysis, it may.

The second methodological issue concerns the accuracy of phonetic transcription. Determining whether a child's imprecise articulation of a phoneme like /ʃ/, for example, should be notated as [s̠], [tˢ], [t̠], [t̠ʃ], and so forth is difficult, and will effect process coding. If "shoe" is transcribed as [tˢu] rather than [tʃu], for example, this sound change will meet the requirements of Palatal Fronting. For these reasons, clinicians should interpret NPA data cautiously, always seeking sufficient replication of an effect within the data, before making important assessment or programming decisions.

If our decision about how to code Palatal Fronting is valid—and *if* the transcription of Toby's speech in this sample is correct—it then *is* valid to say that Toby does not front palatal sounds!

5. Liquid Simplification

Once again, the "O"s entered on the Summary Sheet do not indicate that Toby uses /l/ and /r/ correctly. Rather, because he deletes almost every initial and final /l/ and /r/, he does not use Liquid Simplification. Most interesting here is his correct production of /ɜ/ and /ɚ/. This behavior is of interest theoretically, because it demonstrates that r-colored vowels (/ɝ/ and /ɚ/) can be learned (processed) differently from an r-colored sound functioning as a consonant (/r/). That is, in Toby's speech, vowels and consonants function as different response classes. Toby's production of r-sounds also supports the validity of the symbolization system described for r sounds, as described on page 30. For example, if we had chosen to symbolize final r in monosyllable words as /ɚ/, as some phonetic systems do (for example, as [faɪɚ] rather than [faɪr]) Toby's liquid data would seem more chaotic. That is, Toby deletes /r/s but he does not delete /ɚ/s. Symbolization of r-sounds, as discussed earlier has long been a matter of debate among phoneticians; data like these should provide the most valid bases for symbolization that has clinical utility.

6. Assimilation Processes
Because of Toby's extensive use of deletion as a simplification process, two or more consonants seldom are retained in monosyllable words. As discussed later, one of the management needs is to have him use two lingual consonants in the same word without deleting one or both. If one inspects all the monosyllablic words in the Coding Sheets, only a few words, such as [dʌv] for "stuff," [tʃok] for "coat," and [tʂɑk] for "sock," retained two consonants. Although two-syllable words are not coded for processes other than Unstressed Syllable Deletion on the formal procedure, some of his two-syllable words could be described as evidencing assimilation (for example, [bʌbɚ] for "butter"). As suggested for Stopping, it would be of theoretical interest to observe if Toby's use of assimilation will increase as his deletions abate.

7. Cluster Reduction
Toby's cluster production is best placed at Stage 2, wherein clusters are reduced to one consonant. He does have some correct stop-liquid clusters in initial position, which qualifies as Stage 3 of the four stages of Cluster Reduction described in Appendix A.

8. Unstressed Syllable Deletion
In comparison to other children of his age with delayed speech, Toby's percentage of USD is somewhat higher, but he does mark each syllable approximately 75 percent of the time. Notice that to do so, he uses a glottal stop to replace a variety of consonants. Toby is functioning at Stage 4 of the five stages of Unstressed Syllable Deletion. Inspection of the words in which he deletes a syllable indicates that the present progressive suffix "ing" is sometimes deleted.

To summarize the analysis of developmental stages, Toby's pattern of errors is dominated by deletion of initial and final consonants. His pattern of errors is consistent with others we have seen in children who have a late onset of speech and are delayed in language production.

Context-Function Analysis

Toby's predominant pattern of deletions, both of initial and final consonants, is essentially consistent. Inspection of the Transcription Sheets indicates that only a few non-deletions occur for each sound or for each word that occurs more than once. For example, Toby says final /t/ correctly in "what" whereas he deletes /t/ in all other words. One correct item, however, does not provide enough information for a consistency analysis. Other than some final /n/s that are inconsistently correct—nearly always on the locatives "in" and "on"—we perceive few data that would warrant a context-function analysis. Again, a good exercise for the reader would be to inspect these data to determine whether we have overlooked some potentially interesting associations between context or function variables and sound change.

Implications of NPA data for Management Programming

As indicated by these analyses, Toby is experiencing considerable difficulty in mastering the phonology of his language. His strategy may be nicely contrasted with that of Michael, Case Study 2, who also was a late talker. Whereas Michael's strategy seemed to be "put *something* in" in the face of articulating a word, Toby's strategy might be described as "rather than say something wrong, *delete*." In both cases, these children are undergoing rapid development of pragmatic demands on communication, while searching for the speech behaviors that will allow participation in that communication. Both children seem to be piling up the same phonetic mastery skills, but each uses a different set of phonological simplification strategies to respond to the press to keep talking (Campbell & Shriberg, 1979).

Our suggestions for management follow from consideration of all the NPA data, including these additional analyses. Toby's phonological system might best be aided by working in sequence on two target behaviors: (1) Deletions, and (2) the /s/ phoneme. We summarize here Toby's actual progress over the first four months of a management program.

1. Program 1—Deletion of Final Consonants

A program to reduce final consonant deletions concentrated on teaching Toby *awareness* of final sounds. He was taught to recognize *when* he deleted a final consonant, rather than how to say final sounds. His NPA data indicated that /m/, /n/, and /l/ were in his phonetic inventory. Because these three sounds are earliest emerging in the dissolution of Final Consonant Deletion (Renfrew, 1966; see Appendix A) and because they are voiced continuants (hence they are salient as final sounds in a word) these three sounds were chosen as targets. Stimulus words were characterized by simple canonical structures (CVC's) that contained initial consonants unlikely to trigger Final Consonant Deletion. Emphasis throughout the word-phrase-sentence hierarchy was on self-awareness, self-correction, and self-reinforcement for "putting sounds on the ends of words."

2. Program 2—/s/ Morpheme Program

A variant of an /s/ Morpheme Program (Shriberg & Kwiatkowski, in preparation) was used to impact on Toby's morphophonological development. Toby's NPA data indicated that he was on the verge of *s*-like sounds and his pattern of syntactic development at six years was hindered by final /s/ deletions (Paul and Shriberg, 1979). As developed in a previous case study, Case Study 1: Robby, /s/ may best be taught in word-final position and in grammatical morphemes. Toby progressed from using /s/ as the final sound in a morpheme to /s/ morphemes (plurals, possessives), to other grammatical morphemes requiring /s/. Emphasis once again was on awareness and identification—both in the context of management in school and in a home parent program. Toby's clinician did begin to monitor Toby's exaggerated lip and tongue behaviors associated with /s/ productions, but did not directly teach positional cues for /s/ (recall the discussion of such behaviors in Case Study 2: Michael).

Toby's NPA data, obtained on three occasions in a four-month period reflected his progress on the two programs. The NPA Summary Sheet, which is designed to provide for reliable monitoring of changes across continuous speech samples, was sensitive to Toby's progress. Samples obtained by persons other than his clinician indicated that changes were apparent in four areas. Briefly, (1) Toby's inclusion of final consonants in words increased from 27 to 63 percent,* (2) he began to use Stopping rather than deletion for initial fricative consonants (/s/ had not yet been trained in initial position),

---

* That is, at the outset of management he deleted 11 of the 15 consonants (73 percent) for which there were data on the NPA Summary Sheet (see page 110). On a continuous speech sample obtained less than four months later, he was deleting only 37 percent of final consonants.

(3) correct /s/ began to emerge in final consonant position, but correct /z/ did not (/z/ was as yet untrained), and (4) his percentage of Unstressed Syllable Deletion was reduced from 23 percent at the outset of management to effectively 0 percent. These data are interesting to pursue from a number of theoretical and applied perspectives. Basically here, we view these generalization probes as supportive of the construct validity of NPA procedures as well as NPA's predictive power for planning systematic management.

Some very important questions in management strategies can be approached only by careful monitoring of continuous speech data—to observe the effects of a change in one area of phonology on another area. For example, effect (2) above (the onset of Stopping of fricatives in initial position) is predicted by developmental data. We noticed also that as Toby began to include rather than delete /k/ and /g/, he sometimes used Velar Fronting (that is, [t] and [d]) for these sounds. Should a clinician allow Stopping or Velar Fronting to continue in a situation such as this, or should all sound changes be consequated? The developmental approach would argue for the former, on the assumption that a period of Stopping of initial fricatives or Velar Fronting may be a stage that is *necessary* for the child to pass through. Clinicians might argue for the latter, however, because of concern that in accepting the Stopping or Velar Fronting in a management setting, incorrect articulation might be being reinforced. The problem, of course, relates to the more general issue of what should be taught—and when. Our position simply is that empirical answers to such questions—such as whether the child with delayed speech must recapitulate the normal acquisition sequence—can be obtained only by tracking closely the effects of intervention as reflected in continuous speech samples.

Case Study 4: Kirk

Introduction

This last of the four case studies is adapted from a working paper completed by Rhea Paul. It was one of the first attempts to use the NPA procedure as a research tool. This extended case study is more lengthy than the previous three case studies and organized differently. It is included here because it nicely illustrates the discovery procedures that clinical researchers must undertake to more fully understand associations between speech and language.

NPA Summary Sheet

Following (page 116) is the completed NPA Summary Sheet; other data, including a description of Kirk and examples of his speech are presented within the case study.

Background and Brief Case History

Kirk was five years, nine months at the time of this study. Inspection of free speech transcripts indicated that Kirk uses a variety of phonological processes, but that his phonetic inventory is almost complete. In other words, he is not missing whole classes of sounds, but instead appears to use simplifying processes variably on a wide range of

NPA SUMMARY SHEET

Shriberg and Kwiatkowski
John Wiley & Sons   Copyright 1980 NPA

Child __Kirk__   DOB _____ Age __5-9__
Sampling _____   Analysis _____
Date _____   Date _____
Clinician _____

Total Words _____
Entered _____
(A + B + C) _____

Phonetic Inventory

	m	n	ŋ	w	j	p	b	t	d	k	g	h	f	v	θ	ð	s	z	ʃ	ʒ	tʃ	dʒ	l	r
Correct Anywhere →	x			x	x	x	x	x	x	x	x	x					x							x
Appears Anywhere →	x	x	x	x	x	x		x	x	x	x		x	x	x	x	x	x	x	x		x	x	
Glossed Never Correct →														x							x			
Never Glossed; Never Appears →																								

1 · Final Consonant Deletion

	m	n	ŋ	w	j	p	b	t	d	k	g	h	f	v	θ	ð	s	z	ʃ	ʒ	tʃ	dʒ	l	r
Final Consonant Deletion →	O	O				O	-	∅	∅	∅	∅		✓	∅	O	O	-	O	-	-	-	-	-	∅

2 · Velar Fronting

Initial →	∅	
Final →	∅	

3 · Stopping

Initial →	-	O	-	-	-
Final →	-	∅	-	✓	-

4 · Palatal Fronting

Initial →	∅	
Final →	✓	∅

5 · Liquid Simplification

-	-
-	∅

6 · Progressive Assimilations

Regressive Assimilations

t/w ← d

7 · Cluster Reduction

	Correct	Reduced
Initial Clusters →		s/sk s/st
		f/sp p/pl
Final Clusters →	st nt	t/st d/rz t/ls ∅/md
		n/ns d/ʒz t/lt ∅/nk nd/md

8 · Unstressed Syllable Deletion

	Two Syllable	Three+ Syllable
n	18	8
Deletions n	1	3
% Deletions	6	36

Notes:

* These forms contain only those clusters in which segments do not act as grammatical morphemes. See text, Table 7, for clusters that contain grammatical morphemes.

target sounds. This characteristic of his speech was the main criterion for choosing him as the subject for this study, because it would allow investigation of how grammatical variables interacted with his production of sounds. If he uses phonological processes variably, perhaps some grammatical contexts that increased the probability of process use could be discovered. Another reason for choosing Kirk is that he was enrolled in a speech-language program during the time his most recent speech sample was taken, so that concurrent comprehension and cognitive data were also available.

Records indicated that Kirk was functioning at the late preoperational level of cognitive development at the time of the speech sample. He sorted on two dichotomies without a model, seriated five items, conserved number with a model, counted meaningfully, reproduced circles, squares, and triangles, and sequenced six pictures on a time dimension. This performance for a child of 5−9 indicates that he does not have any significant cognitive delay.

Kirk's language comprehension was tested by means of the *Miller-Yoder (MY) Test of Grammatical Comprehension* (Miller & Yoder, 1980). He responded correctly to all five-year items with the exception of negative/affirmative and singular/plural items. His *Peabody Picture Vocabulary Test* (Dunn, 1965) score yielded a vocabulary age of 6−6.

Program records also indicate that structure and function of the oral mechanism are within normal limits. He was reported to use language for a variety of functions, including commenting, directing, getting information, expressing feelings, pretending, and problem solving. Kirk appears, then, to be a normal five-year old, except in the area of language production.

General Description of Language Production

Two means were used to assess Kirk's productive skills. Miller's procedure (Miller, 1980) was applied to the transcript in order to evaluate Kirk's grammatical development. Shriberg and Kwiatkowski's *NPA* procedure (preliminary version) was used to investigate the general nature of his phonological system.

Kirk's MLU was determined to be 4.75 morphemes per utterance. This places him beyond Brown's Stage V, as one would expect for a child of his age. Structural analysis yielded conflicting results, however. The greatest number of sentences in the sample exemplified structures typical of Stage IV. Miller's mastery criterion would then place Kirk at a Stage IV level of development. This placement represents a significant (more than one stage) discrepancy from MLU. There are a few instances of Stage V structures such as past modals and emphatic *do* in affirmative sentences. He uses a few conjoined and embedded sentences, including relative clauses. No Stage V questions or negations are present. Generally, Kirk makes his sentences long by using prepositional phrases. An analysis of the 14 grammatical morphemes (Brown, 1973; DeVilliers & DeVilliers, 1973) revealed consistent use of *in, on,* and *ing*; absences of marking on plurals and possessives; and inconsistent use of regular past-tense morphemes, regular and irregular third-person singular morphemes, and copulas. Irregular past forms were consistently correct, however (see Table 7). Taken in conjunction with the other structural data alone, these results would appear puzzling because Kirk has failed to master some Stage II (plural) and Stage III (possessive) and Stage V morphemes, yet he performs over 80 percent correctly on articles and irregular past tenses that are placed at V. The relation of this performance to his phonological system must, then, be considered.

A Summary Sheet from the NPA performed on Kirk's transcription is provided on the facing page. It shows that Kirk's phonetic inventory contains correct tokens of most sounds. The low frequency of occurrence of /v/ and /z/ in initial position, where they are more likely to be correct because Kirk uses Stopping only in final position, may account for the absence of these sounds from the sample.

Table 7 Analysis of the 14 grammatical morphemes as they occurred in free speech

Stage	Morpheme	Obligatory Form	Realization	Percent Realized
II	-ing	riding	[rɑɪɪŋ]	100
II	in	in	[ɪn]	100
		in	[ɪn]	100
II	plurals	cheerios	[tɛiou]	0
		spaghettios	[ətɛiou]	
		spaghettios	[ətɛiou]	
III	on	on	[ɔn]	100
		on	[ɔn]	
		on	[ɔ]	
III	possessive	dad's	[dæ]	0
		dad's	[dæ]	
V	irregular past	got	[gɔt]	100
		did	[dɪd]	
V	article	27 instances	22 realizations	81
	regular past	named	[neɪnd]	33
		turned	[tɚ]	
		steered	[siə]	
V	regular third person singular	makes	[meɪt]	0
		puts	[pɪt]	
		puts	[put]	
		melts	[mɛt]	
		hates	[heɪt]	
V	contractible copulas	there's	[ɛəd]	22
		that's	[tæt]	
		am	ø	
		am	ø	
		am	ø	
		That's	[ɑ]	
		there's	[ɪ]	
		that's	[tæpə]	
		what's	[wʌts]	
V+	irregular third-person singular	doesn't	[dɑun]	0

Kirk does make use of a wide range of simplifying processes. He sometimes deletes final /n/, /t/, /d/, /k/, /g/, /r/ and always deletes final /f/ and /v/. He sometimes uses Velar Fronting for /k/ in both initial and final position, and for /g/ in initial position. He always stops final /θ/ and sometimes stops final /s/. Few data were available for initial fricatives; Palatal Fronting sometimes operates on initial /ʃ/. Liquid Simplification occurs sometimes on final /r/ and always on final /l/. Initial sounds are infrequently replaced due to Regressive Assimilation. Initial clusters are often simplified and final clusters often undergo reduction. Six percent of Kirk's two-syllable words are subject to Unstressed Syllable Deletion, while 36 percent of the few three-plus-syllable words are reduced.

Using the NPA to Illuminate the 14 Grammatical Morpheme Analysis

One possible extention of the NPA is to use it as a tool for investigating the relation between the phonological and linguistic constraints operating on Kirk's syntactic system. The 14 grammatical morphemes provide a convenient index for studying this relationship. The question often arises in the clinic as to whether children with production problems are failing to use the grammatical morphemes because they have not yet mastered the syntactic rules for generating them or because their phonological system prohibits the morphemes from being realized. An attempt was made to use the NPA information to address this question in Kirk's speech sample.

Given Kirk's MLU and his overall level of structural development, it is not surprising that he uses the morphemes placed in Stages V and V+ with less than 90 percent accuracy. His failure to use the Stage II plural and Stage III possessive morphemes is puzzling, however, and one might be tempted to attribute the problem to the phonological rather than the linguistic system. But examining the particular phonological contexts for the morphemes in question leads one to a different conclusion.

Two contexts appear for the plural: "cheerios" [tɛiou] and two instances of "spaghettios" [ətɛiou]. Both are polysyllabic words and both require the /z/ form of the plural morpheme. Because /z/ is not present in the inventory, and the NPA deals with consonant deletion only in monosyllabic words, the answer to the question of phonological versus linguistic constraint on morphological development can not be determined from these instances alone. It is certainly possible that whatever Kirk is able to do with monosyllabic words might break down as the words become longer. NPA data show an increase in Unstressed Syllable Deletion from 6 percent in two-syllable words to 36 percent in polysyllables. This suggests that Kirk has trouble with phonological processing as words get longer. So the information from the plural contexts is still ambiguous with regard to the question of the primary limiting factor.

Both instances for the possessive morpheme are the word "dad's," which is simplified to [dæ]. Inspection of the NPA data reveals that most final clusters are reduced and that all final clusters containing /s/ are reduced with the exception of the words "last" and "what's." But these examples show that Kirk is capable of producing a final cluster containing /s/. Kirk's articulation of "there's" [ɛɑd] is also instructive. Here he has deleted the morpheme final /r/, a process he sometimes uses in other final /r/ contexts in CVC's, and added a copula morpheme realized as Stopped [d]. There is nothing in the transcript to indicate that Kirk ever replaces /r/ with [d]. But there is ample evidence that he often stops fricatives in the final position. This example, too, implies that even if Kirk had used Final Consonant Deletion to omit the /d/ of "dad," he is still capable of adding a morpheme after the process had taken place. (Although if this had been the sequence of operations it would have produced [dæd], which would have appeared to be unmarked). Formally, NPA does not allow for rule ordering, however this kind of analysis is quite within the scope of additional context-function analyses. This sort of reasoning from the evidence is necessary to attack questions of language/speech interaction, because they are so difficult to answer directly.

A conclusion from this analysis would be that, at least in the case of monosyllabic words Kirk's phonological system would allow him to mark plural and possessives in some way. This is based on evidence from his marking of copulas with similar phonological contexts. It would seem that there is at least an *interaction* between the limits placed on production by the phonological and the syntactic systems. Examinations of phonological processes and morphological contexts leads to the conclusion that it is not only Kirk's phonology that keeps him from realizing early grammatical morphemes. There appears to be a linguistic constraint, as well.

The regular third-person provides a similar example. Kirk sometimes supplies the /s, z/ morpheme when a copula is required, but never adds it for the third person singular, although the phonological contexts are exactly analogous. He realizes "what's" as [wʌts], but "puts," "makes," and "hates" are never marked. Again it appears that there is at least an interaction between phonological and grammatical constraints, because Kirk's phonology alone does not preclude the production of marked third person singular forms.

It is also worth noting that of the copula forms that do appear, all involve some marking of the 's or *is,* while the phonologically simpler *am* never appears. This fact adds additional strength to the argument that it is grammatical, not phonological forms that Kirk is in the process of mastering.

This analysis of the relation between Kirk's phonological and linguistic system leads to the conclusion that it is not only the phonological disorder that limits Kirk's use of grammatical morphemes. Taken together with the relatively simple structure of most of his sentences, and the fact that he missed singular/plural items on the MY comprehension test, it is possible to argue that Kirk has a syntactic delay that interacts with his phonological problem to restrict his ability to generate grammatical morphemes. Using the NPA to examine the particular phonological contexts for these morphemes appears to be a very promising approach to illuminating the interaction.

Comparing Grammatical Complexity and Phonological Process Use

Another way of looking at the interaction between language and speech development is suggested by the DeVilliers and DeVilliers (1978) study of processes used in the one- and two-word stage. Their results showed that as words for which simplification processes had ceased to operate in single-word utterances were first used in two-word combinations, the old simplifying processes functioned again on words in the new structural context. One way to look at the relation between syntactic and phonological development is to examine whether the same principle applies at later stages in a phonologically disordered child. The hypothesis would be that the more complex sentences would require a greater number of simplification processes than would simple sentences. Because this study is cross-sectional rather than longitudinal, as was the DeVilliers', a distinction between *old* and *new* surface forms cannot be made. Each sentence was assigned to the highest grammatical stage that the structures within it indicated and the percentage of words in the sentence that underwent simplification processes was counted. Sentences that could not be assigned reliably were excluded. The results are summarized in Table 8. Apparently, increasing complexity of the sentence is not associated with an overall increase in the number of words that are reduced by simplification processes. An average of 51 percent of the words in Stage II sentences and 49 percent of the words in Stage III sentences were simplified while an average of only 34 percent of the words in Stage IV sentences and 29 percent of the words in Stage V sentences were simplified. It appears, then, that for Kirk, the clear sacrifice of phonological accuracy in the service of recent syntactic acquisitions does

Table 8 Analysis of grammatical complexity and simplification processes

Structural Stage	Number of Sentences	Average Percentage of Words in the Sentence That Underwent Simplification
II	9	51
III	15	43
IV	26	34
V	7	29

not operate at this later stage of language production, at least not at the rather crude level of this analysis.

An attempt was made to find a more sensitive measure with which to investigate the relation between Kirk's language and the sound system. Each word (type) in the transcript and each appearance of the word (token) was scored both for whether it underwent some simplification process (regardless of which process it was), and for the stage assignment of the sentence in which the token appeared. This method would hopefully reveal whether the articulation of particular words was vulnerable to the effects of grammatical complexity of the ambient sentence.

Preliminary inspection of the data revealed that the overwhelming majority of the tokens (92 percent) were either always right or always wrong for a particular type. This was true when the tokens appeared in a variety of sentences with a range of complexity. Again it seemed that it was not the syntax of the sentences that was controlling phonological production. A search then was made for some other explanation. The types were classified by the canonical structures utilized in the NPA and the percentage of simplification within each category was examined. Table 9 summarizes the results of this analysis.

Effect of Canonical Structure

Canonical structure may have some effect on the probability of the use of simplification process, but not as much effect as do the particular target sounds. The CV syllable, considered by Jakobson (1968) to be the most basic, is never simplified in 81 percent of the words with that structure. Of the three words (19 percent) in this category that are simplified, one contains a velar ("go") and another a fricative ("she"). Both these

Table 9 Associations among canonical structures and phonological simplifications

Canonical Structure		Number of Types	Percentage of Types Simplified		
			"Never"	"Always"	"Sometimes"
CV	(all CV's)	16	81	19	0
	(including only front stops, nasals, and glides)	14	93	7	0
	(including velars and fricatives)	2	0	100	0
VC	(all VC's)	10	40	50	10
	(including only front stops and nasals)	6	67	17	17
	(including fricatives and liquids)	4	0	100	0
CVC	(all CVC's)	42	38	52	10
	(including only front stops and nasals)	8	75	25	0
	(including velar, fricative, and liquids)	34	29	59	12
clusters	(in monosyllables)	23	0	87	13
polysyllabic words		18	11	78	11

sounds are variably correct, according to Kirk's NPA. The words that are always correct contain only front stops, nasals, and glides. In the case of VC's, only 40 percent of the total are never simplified. However, when these are divided into words that contain only front stops and nasals, sounds on which Kirk's simplifying processes rarely operate—versus those that contain fricatives—clearer results emerge. Of those VC's containing only front stops and nasals, 67 percent are never simplified. Of those containing fricatives, or liquids, *all* are *always* simplified. A similar finding emerges for CVC's. When taken together only 38 percent of the CVC's are never simplified. But grouping the words by the type of sounds they contain again reveals differences. The CVC's containing only front stops and nasals are much more likely never to be simplified (75 percent of the words in this group) than are those containing the velars, fricatives, and liquids (29 percent of these words are never simplified).

Monosyllable types containing clusters are always simplified in at least some of their tokens. Only 11 percent of the polysyllable words are never simplified in Kirk's transcript. It appears then that those processes that Kirk uses, Velar Fronting, Stopping, Liquid Simplification, and Cluster Reduction, operate across canonical types. Neither syntactic or syllable structure has a very powerful affect on Kirk's use of simplification.

Conclusions

This analysis shows Kirk to be a child who makes heavy use of simplification processes that operate on velar, fricative, and liquid phonemes. Neither grammatical or canonical structures interact very strongly with process use. But the phonological analysis also helps to highlight Kirk's language problems. Comparison of his 14 morpheme analysis with the NPA data indicates that he is capable of producing sound combinations similar to those required in the morphological contexts. Therefore his phonological system is not the only factor limiting the production of grammatical morphemes. This fact, combined with a structural analysis of his sentences, implies that Kirk has a productive language delay in addition to his phonological disorder.

There is no reason to believe that Kirk's pattern will be typical of all children with phonological disorders. For some children, the interactions between language and speech development, and between process use and canonical structure, may be more powerful than they are for Kirk. The purpose of this study has been to explore the use of phonological process analysis as a tool for clarifying some of the questions that arise in the clinical evaluation of children suspected of having language and speech disorders. It seems that the NPA and inferences made from it provides a very promising instrument for examining relations between and among speech and language skills—and for diagnosing language delay with greater confidence in children whose phonological disabilities make such diagnosis difficult.

References

Unpublished Working Papers (with Student/Staff Participants)

1975 Preliminaries to Natural Process Analysis (J. Brooks, D. Dinan, M. Goodman)

1976 Development of a Procedure for Description of Phonological Processes (J. Jordan)

1976 Imitative Versus Spontaneous Tests Responses: Implications for Natural Process Analysis (C. Caldwell)

1976 A Procedure for Natural Process Analysis (NPA): The Test and Preliminary Data (K. Corbett, M. Bruening, K. Carlson)

1977 Natural Process Analysis (NPA) of a Longitudinal Sample of Children with Delayed Speech (R. Garrison, K. Laird, J. Trigiani)

1977 A Study of Natural Process Analysis (NPA) in Fifteen Normal Children (E. Eide)

1977 Comparison of Phonological Processes Using the PAT Versus Spontaneous Speech Performances (S. Bezack, L. Forner)

1978 A Preliminary Review of Variables Affecting Unstressed Syllable Deletion (P. Boren, S. Dravininkas)

1978 A Comparison of the Use of Multisyllable Words and Parts of Speech in the Free Speech of Normal and Phonologically Delayed Children (B. Becher, P. Wright)

1978 Disambiguating Natural Process Usage (J. Baran, T. Yonick)

1978 Interrelationships Between Children's Phonological and Language Behaviors (N. Ouwens)

1978 Normal Phonological Development (K. Green)

1978 Reliability, Efficiency, and Validity of a Nonsense Word Test of Phonological Processes (K. Carlson)

1978 A Study of Procedures for Supplementary Analysis of NPA Data (P. Light)

1979 A Second Look at Polysyllabic Words Coded by the NPA Procedure (P. Porter)

References

Anderson, S. *The Organization of Phonology.* New York: Academic Press (1974).

Anthony, A., Boyle, D., Ingram, T., and McIsaac, M. *The Edinburgh Articulation Test.* Edinburgh, Scotland: E and S Livingstone (1971).

Atkinson-King, K. Children's acquisition of phonological stress contrasts. UCLA Working Papers in Phonetics, 25 (1973).

Barrie-Blackley, S., Musselwhite, C., and Rogister, S. *Clinical Oral Language Sampling: A Handbook for Clinicians*. S. Hadjian, (Ed.) Sponsored by the National Student Speech and Hearing Association, Danville, Ill.: Interstate Printers (1978).

Berko, J. The child's learning of English morphology. *Word* 14, 150−177 (1958).

Bloom, L., and Lahey, M. *Language Development and Language Disorders*. New York: Wiley (1978).

Brannigan, G. Syllabic structure and the acquisition of consonants: the great conspiracy in word formation. *Journal of Psycholinguistic Research* 15, 117−133 (1976).

Brown, R. *A First Language*. Cambridge: Harvard University Press (1973).

Campbell, T., and Shriberg, L. Effect of pragmatic structures on phonological production in speech-delayed children. Paper presented at the American Speech and Hearing Association National Convention, Atlanta, November (1979).

Carterette, E., and Jones, M. *Informal Speech: Alphabetic and Phonemic Texts with Statistical Analyses and Tables*. Berkeley: University of California Press (1974).

Compton, A. Generative studies of children's phonological disorders. *Journal of Speech and Hearing Disorders* 35, 315−339 (1970).

Compton, A. Generative studies of children's phonological disorders: a strategy of therapy. In S. Singh (Ed.) *Measurement in Speech and Hearing*. Baltimore: University Park Press (1975).

Compton, A., and Streeter, M. Studies of early child phonology: data collection and preliminary analyses. *Papers and Reports in Child Language Development* Stanford University, 13, 99−109 (1977).

Costley, M., and Broen, P. The nature of listener disagreement in judging misarticulated speech. Paper presented at the American Speech and Hearing Association National Convention, Houston, November (1976).

DeVilliers, J., and DeVilliers, P. A cross-sectional study of the acquisition of grammatical morphemes in child speech. *Journal of Psycholinguistic Research* 2, 267−278 (1973).

DeVilliers, P., and Devilliers, J. Simplifying phonological processes in the one- and two-word stage. Paper presented at Boston University Conference on Child Language Development (1978).

Dubois, E., and Bernthal, J. A comparison of three methods for obtaining articulatory responses. *Journal of Speech and Hearing Disorders* 43, 295−305 (1978).

Dunn, L. *The Peabody Picture Vocabulary Test*. Circle Pines, Minn. American Guidance Service, Inc. (1965).

Edwards, M. Perception and production in child phonology: the testing of four hypothesis. *Journal of Child Language* 1, 205−219 (1974).

Edwards, M., and Garnica, O. Patterns of variation in the repetition of utterances by young children. Unpublished paper, Stanford University (1973).

Faircloth, M., and Dickerson, M. Conversational speech analyses. A short course presented at the American Speech and Hearing Association National Convention, Chicago, November (1977).

Faircloth, M., and Faircloth, S. An analysis of the articulatory behavior of a speech defective child in connected speech and in isolated word responses. *Journal of Speech and Hearing Disorders* 35, 51−61 (1970).

Ferguson, C., and Farwell, C. Words and sounds in early language acquisition: English initial consonants in the first fifty words. *Language* 51, 419−439 (1975).

Ferguson, C., and Garnica, O. Theories of phonological development. In E. Lenneberg and E. Lenneberg (Eds.) *Foundations Of Language Development*. UNESCO.

Fisher, H., and Logemann, J. *The Fisher-Logemann Test of Articulation Competence*. New York: Houghton Mifflin (1971).

Foley, J. *Foundations of Theoretical Phonology*. Cambridge Studies in Linguistics, 20. Cambridge: Cambridge University Press (1977).

Fromkin, V. *Speech Errors as Linguistic Evidence*. The Hague: Mouton (1973).

Garnica, O., and Edwards, M. Phonological variation in children's speech: the trade-off phenomenon. *Ohio State University Working Papers in Linguistics* 22, 81−87 (1977).

Goldman, R., and Fristoe, M. *Test of Articulation*. Circle Pines, Minn.: American Guidance Service (1969).

Greenlee, M. Interacting processes in the child's acquisition of stop-liquid clusters. *Papers and Reports on Child Language Development*, 85−100 (1974).

Gruber, J. Preverbal vocalization. In C. Ferguson and D. Slobin (Eds.) *Studies of Child Language Development*. New York: Holt, Rhinehart and Winston (1973).

Hare, G., and Irwin, J. Consonant acquisition in children aged 21−24 months. Paper presented at the American Speech and Hearing Association National Convention, San Francisco, November (1978).

Hejna, R. *Hejna Developmental Articulation Test*. Madison: Wisconsin College of Typing (1955).

Hodson, B. A preliminary hierarchical model for phonological remediation. *Language, Speech, Hearing Services in Schools* 9, 236−240 (1978).

Hooper, J. *An Introduction to Natural Generative Phonology*. New York: Academic Press (1976).

Ingram, D. *Phonological Disability in Children*. New York: Elsevier (1976).

Irwin, O. Infant speech: consonantal sounds according to place of articulation. *Journal of Speech and Hearing Disorders* 12, 397−401 (1951).

Jakobson, R. *Child Language, Aphasia, and Phonological Universals*. The Hague: Mouton (1968).

Kenstowicz, M., and Kisseberth, C. *Topics in Phonological Theory*. New York: Academic Press (1977).

Kent, R. Anatomical and neuromuscular maturation of the speech mechanism: evidence from acoustic studies. *Journal of Speech and Hearing Research* 19, 421−447 (1976).

Kenyon, J., and Knott, T. *A Pronouncing Dictionary of American English*. Springfield, Mass.: Merriam (1953).

Kiparsky, P. How abstract is phonology? Unpublished paper (1968).

Klein, H. The relationship between perceptual strategies and productive strategies in learning the phonology of early lexical items. Bloomington: Indiana University Linguistics Club (1978).

Koutsoudas, A., Sanders, G., and Noll, C. The application of phonological rules. *Language* 50, 1−28 (1974).

Ladefoged, P. *A Course in Phonetics*. New York: Harcourt Brace Jovanovich (1975).

Leonard L., Schwartz, R., Folger, M., and Wilcox, M. Some aspects of child phonology in imitative and spontaneous speech. *Journal of Child Language*, (in press).

Leopold, W. *Speech Development of a Bilingual Child: a Linguist's Record 2. Sound-Learning in the First Two Years*. Evanston, Ill.: Northwestern University Press (1947).

Locke, J. The prediction of child speech errors: implications for a theory of acquisition.

NICHD Conference on *Child Phonology: Perception, Production and Deviation.* Bethesda, May (1978).

Macken, M. The child's lexical representation: evidence from the *"puzzle-puddle-pickle"* phenomenon. Mimeo. Stanford University (1978a).

Macken, M. Aspects of the acquisition of stop systems: a cross-linguistic perspective. NICHD Conference on *Child Phonology: Perception, Production, and Deviation.* Bethesda, May (1978b).

McReynolds, L., and Elbert, M. Procedures for a phonological analyses of children's articulation errors. Short course presented at the American Speech and Hearing Association National Convention, San Francisco, November (1978).

McReynolds, L., and Engmann, D. *Distinctive Feature Analyses of Misarticulations.* Baltimore: University Park Press (1975).

Menn, L. Phonological theory and child phonology. NICHD Conference on *Child Phonology: Perception, Production, and Deviation,* Bethesda, May (1978).

Menyuk, P. The role of distinctive features in children's acquisition of phonology. *Journal of Speech and Hearing Disorders* 11, 138−146 (1968).

MacKay, I. *Practical Phonetics.* Boston: Little, Brown (1978).

Miller, J., (Ed.) *Assessing Language Production in Children: Experimental Procedures.* Baltimore: University Park Press (1980).

Miller, J., and Yoder, D. *The MY Test.* In J. Miller (Ed.) *Assessing Language Production in Children: Experimental Procedures.* Baltimore: University Park Press (1980).

Miller-Donnegan, P. Some context-free processes affecting vowels. In A. Zwicky (Ed.) *Working Papers in Linguistics* 11, Ohio State University, 136−167 (1972).

Morse, P. Infant speech perception: a preliminary model and review of the literature. In R. Schiefelbusch and L. Lloyd (Eds.) *Language Perspectives-Acquisition, Retardation, and Intervention.* Baltimore: University Park Press (1974).

Moskowitz, A. The two-year-old stage in the acquisition of English phonology. *Language* 46, 426−441 (1970).

Noll, J. Articulation assessment. In J. Fricke (Ed.) *Speech and the Dentofacial Complex: The State of the Art.* ASHA Reports No. 5, Washington D.C., American Speech and Hearing Association, October (1970).

Ohala, J. Phonetic explanation in phonology. In *Parasession on Natural Phonology,* Chicago Linguistic Society, 251−274 (1974).

Oller, D. Simplification as the goal of phonological processes in child speech. *Language Learning* 24, 299−303 (1975).

Oller, D., Wiemans, L., Doyle, W., and Ross, C. Child speech, babbling, and phonological universals. *Papers and Reports in Child Language Development* 8, 33−41 (1974).

Olmsted, D. *Out of the Mouth of Babes.* The Hague: Mouton (1971).

Paul, R., and Shriberg, L. Associations between phonology and morphology in speech-delayed children. Paper presented at the American Speech and Hearing Association National Convention, Atlanta, November (1979).

Pendergast, K., Dickey, S., Selmar, J., and Soder, A. *The Photo Articulation Test.* 2nd Ed. Danville, Ill.: The Interstate Press (1969).

Peters, J., and Lauffer, M. Acoustic phonetics in the clinic: a case study. Paper presented at the American Speech and Hearing Association National Convention, Houston, November (1976).

Piaget, J. *Play, Dreams, and Imitation in Childhood.* New York: Norton (1962).

Powers, M. Functional disorders of articulation: symptomatology and etiology. In L. Travis (Ed.) *The Handbook of Speech Pathology and Audiology*. New York: Prentice-Hall (1971).

Prather, E., Hedrick, D., and Kern, C. Articulation development in children aged two to four years. *Journal of Speech and Hearing Disorders* 40, 179–191 (1975).

Renfrew, C. Persistence of the open syllable in defective articulation. *Journal of Speech and Hearing Disorders* 31, 370–373 (1966).

Roberts, A. *A Statistical Linguistic Analysis of American English*. The Hague: Mouton (1965).

Sander, E. When are speech sounds learned? *Journal of Speech and Hearing Disorders* 37, 55–63 (1972).

Schwartz, R., and Folger, M. Phonological behavior in normal and language disordered children. Paper presented at the American Speech and Hearing Association National Convention, Chicago, November (1977).

Shriberg, L. Articulation judgments: some perceptual considerations. *Journal of Speech and Hearing Research* 15, 876–882 (1972).

Shriberg, L. A response evocation program for /ɝ/. *Journal of Speech and Hearing Disorders* 40, 92–105 (1975).

Shriberg, L. Reviews of the *Riley Articulation and Language Test* and the *Photo Articulation Test*. In O. Buros (Ed.) Eighth Mental Measurements Yearbook. Highland Park, N.J.: The Institute of Mental Measurements (1978).

Shriberg, L. An intervention procedure for children with persistent /r/ errors. *Language, Speech, and Hearing Services in Schools* (in press).

Shriberg, L. Developmental phonological disorders. Chapter 7 in T. Hixon, L. Shriberg, and J. Saxman (Eds). *Introduction to Communication Disorders*. Englewood Cliffs: Prentice-Hall (1980).

Shriberg, L., and Kent, R. *Clinical Phonetics*. (In preparation).

Shriberg, L., and Kwiatkowski, J. Phonological programming for unintelligible children in early childhood projects. Paper presented at the American Speech and Hearing Association National Convention, Chicago, November (1977).

Shriberg, L., and Kwiatkowski, J. Natural process analysis for children with severely delayed speech. Paper presented at the American Speech and Hearing Association National Convention, San Francisco, November (1978).

Shriberg, L., and Kwiatkowski, J. A diagnostic classification system for developmental phonological disorders (in submission).

Shriberg, L., Lotz, W., and Carlson, K. Effects of child, clinician, and audio recording variables on the efficiency of MLU transcription: (in preparation).

Shriberg, L., and Smith, A. Phonological indices of middle ear involvement in speech-delayed children (in submission).

Shriberg, L., and Swisher, W. Development of an articulation scoring training program (ASTP). Paper presented at the American Speech and Hearing Association National Convention, San Francisco, November (1972).

Shvachkin, N. The development of phonemic speech perception in early childhood. In C. Ferguson and D. Slobin (Eds.) *Studies of Child Language Development*. New York: Holt, Rhinehart and Winston (1973).

Smith, N. Lexical representation and the acquisition of phonology. Forum lecture, Linguistic Institute of the Linguistic Society of America, Urbana, Ill. (1978).

Sommerstein, A. *Modern Phonology*. Baltimore: University Park Press (1977).

Stark, R., Rose, N., and McLagen, M. The features of infant sounds: the first eight weeks of life. *Journal of Child Language* 2, 205–221 (1975).

Stampe, D. The acquisition of phonetic representation. Papers from the Fifth Regional Meeting, Chicago Linguistic Society (1969).

Stampe, D. A dissertation on natural phonology. Unpublished doctoral dissertation, University of Chicago (1973).

Templin, M. *Certain Language Skills in Children*. Minneapolis: The University of Minnesota Press (1957).

Templin, M., and Darley, F. *The Templin Darley Tests of Articulation*. 2nd Ed., Iowa City: Bureau of Educational Research and Service, Division of Extension and University Services, University of Iowa (1969).

Weiner, F. *Phonological Process Analysis*. Baltimore: University Park Press (1978).

Weiner, F., and Bernthal, J. Articulation feature assessment. In S. Singh and J. Lynch (Eds.) *Diagnostic Procedures in Hearing Speech and Language*. Baltimore: University Park Press (1978).

Weismer, G., Dinnsen, D., and Elbert, M. A clinical study of the voicing distinction and final stop deletion. Indiana University Linguistics Club (1979).

Wepman, J., and Hass, W. *A Spoken Word Count*. Chicago: Language Research Associates (1969).

Winitz, H. *Articulatory Acquisition and Behavior*. New York: Prentice-Hall (1969).

Wolff, P. The natural history of crying and other vocalizations in early infancy. In B. Foss (Ed.) *Determinants of Infant Behavior*. IV. London: Methuen (1969).

APPENDIX A

Acquisition of Phonology

How To Use This Appendix

Normative data on phonological development currently are being gathered in a number of large-scale studies. To date, however, the single best description of normal and delayed speech development is provided by Ingram (1976). Rather than attempt piecemeal revisions of Ingram's synthesis, this outline will adhere closely to Ingram's review, including his description of phonological processes. Therefore, the data presented here should be viewed as only a working framework for an NPA analysis. The reader will want to update this outline as emerging literature and clinical experience warrant. We have found it useful to log marginal notes beside tabled entries as each NPA analysis supports or fails to support a given entry.* As the results of longitudinal studies currently underway in several research centers become available, this brief sketch of normal phonological development will undoubtedly require a major overhaul.

Ingram's conception of the stages of phonological development are presented in Table 10. As discussed in the text, the major period within this scheme is Stage III, Phonology of the Simple Morpheme. Stage III includes the period of phonological development in which most of the phonological simplification processes are observed. For ease of reference in the outline here, *all* phonological processes—even those that assumedly occur in Stage II and those that persist into Stage IV—are discussed in the section for Stage III. In using these entries for the purposes of an NPA ananlysis, it is important to keep in mind the following factors.

1. Only phonological processes described by Ingram are included in this outline. Ingram's inventory of processes includes many more than the eight coded in the NPA procedures. As discussed in the text, many of the processes observed early in normal acquisition are seldom observed clinically, while others are difficult to transcribe reliably. Nevertheless, these additional processes may be useful for the purposes of particular phonological analyses (such as for younger children or for children with other disabilities). The clinician should be alert to data that confirm or fail to support the reality and clinical utility of processes other than the eight coded in the NPA.

2. Some of Ingram's examples will appear to involve arbitrary process coding, that is, the sound change could be attributed to any of several processes. This is of little consequence here, but such examples demonstrate why NPA restricts process coding in several ways so as to minimize such data. As developed in the text, the linguist is trained to view sound-change data as reflecting a number of assumptions about the organization of phonology. Indeed, developing alternative rationales for particular analyses of sound change is one of the things that linguists do. The speech-language pathologist, however, must greatly simplify the task of discovering the major processes underlying the child's surface forms. The NPA accomplishes this end primarily by one simple expedient: neither multiple processes nor ordered rules are allowed.

3. Process Stage Analysis, as discussed in Part III and illustrated in the case examples, will require data included on the following pages (for convenience here, ordered as they occur on the NPA Summary Sheet)†:
   Final Consonant Deletion — 137

---

* For example, we have begun to doubt the generalizability of Renfrew's (1966) data on the dissolution of Final Consonant Deletion in children with delayed speech (see for example, Case Study 2 and Case Study 3). Recent data on stop acquisition in normal development (Macken, 1978b) resolves many puzzling discrepancies between Renfrew's stage data and our clinical observations of children with delayed speech. Wherever available, however, we prefer to draw from studies of clinical samples; Renfrew's study is one of the few available sources of data on children with delayed speech.

† For ease of reference, each of these eight natural processes coded in the NPA procedure are set in bold face type in the body of the appendix.

0 to 12 Months Stage 1: Prelinguistic Vocalization and Perception

A. Crying—beginning with the birth cry and characterized by (Stark et al., 1975; Wolff, 1969):
  1. Sequence—short cry (1 sec.), rest, inspiration, and rest.
  2. Duration—cycle repeats for up to 30 seconds.
  3. Eggressive direction of air.
  4. Voiced.
  5. Harsh.
  6. Rapidly changing pitch variations.
     a. Mad cry—loud and turbulent.
     b. Pain cry—longer duration.

B. Discomfort Sounds—characterized by:
  1. Less stress than for crying, i.e., occurs when the infant can not reach something he or she wants.
  2. Shorter duration than the cry.
  3. Less harshness.
  4. More consonantal than vocalic (open) as in crying; more liquids, nasals, and sonorants.

C. Vegetative Sounds—coughing, burping, sucking, grunting sounds and sighs—characterized by:
  1. Brief duration.
  2. Consonantal—stops, fricatives, and clicks.
  3. Lack of voicing—sounds are faint.
  4. Ingressive direction of air.

D. Cooing—begins to occur at about 2 to 3 months and is concurrent with social smiling and an increase in the diversity of sounds. Cooing also seems to be the first vocal expression of pleasure (Ingram, 1976), can be elicited, and can be observed following feeding. Characterized by:
  1. Sounds are largely vocalics.
  2. Increasing number of back consonantal sounds—velars and glottals become predominant (Winitz, 1969; Irwin, 1951).
  3. Less crying is occurring.
  4. The child can discriminate perceptually between two sounds (Morse, 1974).
  5. Vocalizations may be imitative attempts—vocal contagion first, and later the infant imitates own productions (Piaget, 1962).

E. Babbling—begins to occur at about 5 to 6 months and is predominant up to about 12 months. Babbling, defined as vocalization possessing at least one vowel and one consonant, is characterized by:
  1. Sounds are becoming more "speech-like."
  2. Labial consonants are becoming more frequent than velars.
  3. Singleton consonants, not clusters (Oller et al., 1974).
  4. CV, VC syllables, with CV more common (Oller et al., 1974).

Table 10 Piaget's cognitive stages of development with approximate ages, and the grammatical and phonological stages that correspond to each.

Piaget's Stages	Linguistic Stages	Phonological Stages
Sensori-motor period (0;0−1;6) Development of systems of movements and perception. Child achieves notion of object permanence.	1 Prelinguistic communication through gestures and crying. 2 Holophrastic stage. Use of one-word utterances.	1 Prelinguistic vocalization and perception (birth to 1;0). 2 Phonology of the first 50 words (1;0−1;6).
Period of concrete operations (1;6−12;0) Preconcept subperiod (1;6−4;0). The onset of symbolic representation. Child can now refer to past and future, although most activity is in the here and now. Predominance of symbolic play.	3 Telegraphic stage. Child begins to use words in combinations. These increase to point between 3 and 4 when most sentences become close to well-formed, simple sentences.	3 Phonology of single morphemes. Child begins to expand inventory of speech sounds. Phonological processes that result in incorrect productions predominate until around age 4 when most words of simple morphological structure are correctly spoken.
Intuitional subperiod (4;0−7;0). Child relies on immediate perception to solve various tasks. Begins to develop the concept of reversibility. Child begins to be involved in social games.	4 Early complex sentences. Child begins to use complements on verbs and some relative clauses. These early complex structures, however, appear to be the result of juxtaposition.	4 Completion of the phonetic inventory. The child acquires production of troublesome sounds by age 7. Good production of simple words. Beginning of use of longer words.
Concrete operations subperiod (7;0−12;0). Child learns the notion of reversibility. Can solve tasks dealing with conservation of mass, weight, and volume.	5 Complex sentences. Child acquires the transformational rules that embed one sentence into another. Coordination of sentences decreases, v. the increase in complex sentences.	5 Morphophonemic development. Child learns more elaborate derivational structure of the language; acquires morphophonemic rules of language.
Period of formal operations (12;0−16;0). Child learns the ability to use abstract thought. Can solve problems through reflection.	6 Linguistic intuitions. Child can now reflect upon grammaticality of his or her speech and arrive at linguistic intuitions.	6 Spelling. Child masters ability to spell.

5. Repetitive syllables (reduplication)—[bababa] (Ingram, 1976).
6. Initial consonants (CV) are deaspirated stops (Oller et al., 1974).
7. Final consonants (VC) are devoiced (Oller et al., 1974).
8. Consonants in final position are fricatives (Oller et al., 1974).
9. Fronting becomes predominant (Oller et al., 1974).
10. Increasing markedness (addition of features) from the beginning of the utterance to the end (Gruber, 1973).
11. Diverse sounds, including rare phonetic elements, are produced—for example, bilabial trill, syllabic nasals (Oller et al., 1974).
12. More glides than liquids (Oller et al., 1974).

13. Vocalizations do not yet appear to have lexical meaning.
14. Imitation of others' productions; overall imitative ability is increasing ("vocalized play").

1-0 to 1-6. Stage II: Phonology of the First 50 Words

Transition from prelinguistic babbling to this stage usually involves a decrease in the variety of sounds produced by the child and a subsequent increase in the production of specific sounds (especially consonants) from which the child constructs his or her first 50 meaningful words through selective imitation of adult words. Although babbling may still occur, it easily can be distinguished from the more lexically oriented productions that now are beginning to occur. This stage is characterized by

1. The first syllables are open (CV) and reduplicated (CVCV) (Brannigan, 197 Jakobson, 1968).
2. The first consonants usually are front stops—/p/, /t/, and /b/—/m/ also is common.
3. Some children begin with velars (Ingram, 1976).
4. /h/ and /w/ often are among the first sounds produced (Ferguson and Garnica, 1975).
5. The first vowel used is /a/; /i/ and /u/ follow.
6. A homorganic fricative is acquired only after the stop (Ingram, 1976; Jakobson, 1968).
7. High variation in word forms for individual children (Ferguson and Farwell, 1975).
8. More accurate forms of a word are produced as learning proceeds, but advanced forms ("progressive idioms") also have been reported (Leopold, 1947), e.g., [prɪtɪ]→[pʃɪti]→[pɪti]→[bɪdi].
9. Words attempted are selectively chosen (Ferguson and Farwell, 1975).
10. Trade-off—acquisition of a new part of a word may distort production of the old part (Edwards and Garnica, 1973).
11. Imitation is still limited to forms with which the child can cope (Ingram, 1976).
12. Vocabulary is small, and there does not yet appear to be a productive sound system (Ingram, 1976).
13. Perceptual ability to discriminate words and their meanings develops gradually with the development of phonemic perception (1-0 to 2-0 years). This process may not yet be complete by 2 years (Ingram, 1976). Perceptual ability generally is thought to precede production of the words involved (Edwards, 1974).

1-6 to 4-0. Stage III: Phonology of the Simple Morpheme

This is a period when the child is developing his or her perceptual abilities, acquiring a larger inventory of phonetic elements, gradually losing some simplifying phonological processes, and acquiring a phonological system of contrasts. Consequently, the child's vocabulary grows very rapidly (Ingram, 1976).

A. Perception—A hierarchy of phonemic perceptual contrasts develops with a trend from the more general to the more elaborate (Shvachkin, 1973).
   1. Sequence of distinctions among vowels.
      a. /a/ versus other vowels.
      b. /i/−/u/, /e/−/u/, /i/−/o/, /e/−/o/.
      c. /i/−/e/, /e/−/u/.

2. Distinction of the presence of consonants: bʊk/−/ʊk/, etc.
3. Distinction of sonorants and voiced stops: /m/−/b/, /r/−/d/, etc.
4. Distinction of palatalized and nonpálatalized consonants (found in Shvachkin's Russian children, but not in English children).
5. Distinction of sonorants.
    a. Nasals versus liquids (glides): /m/−/l/, /n/−/j/
    b. /m/−/n/.
    c. /l/−/r/.
    d. Sonorants versus continuants: /m/−/z/, etc.
6. Distinction of obstruents.
    a. Labials versus linguals: /b/−/d/, /b/−/g/, /v/−/z/, etc.
    b. Stops versus spirants: /b/−/v/, /t/−/s/, etc.
    c. Pre- versus postlinguals: /d/−/g/, etc.
    d. Voiced versus voiceless consonants: /p/−/b/, /t/−/d/, /k/−/g/, /s/−/z/, etc.
    e. Between sibilants: /ʒ/−/z/, /ʃ/−/s/, etc.
    f. Liquids versus /j/; /r/−/j/, /l/−/j/.

B. Phonetic Elements (Ingram, 1976).
    1. Vowels are all acquired by 3 years.
    2. Consonants are acquired as follows.
        a. Generally acquired in initial position first, then medial, then final.
        b. Nasals all acquired first.
        c. Glides all acquired next.
        d. Then stops are acquired, except /t/.
        e. Fricatives and affricates are yet incomplete.
    3. Consonant clusters begin to be acquired (Ingram, 1976; Templin, 1957).
        a. Initial position clusters.
            (1) /s/ + nasal—/sm/, /sn/.
            (2) /s/ + stop—/sp/, /st/, /sk/.
            (3) stop + liquid—/pl/, /pr/, /gl/, /kr/.
            (4) stop + glide—/tw/, /kw/.
        b. Final position clusters.
            (1) liquid + stop—/lp/, /lt/.
            (2) liquid + nasal—/rm/.
    4. Stops in the initial position are the most stable; final stops are least stable.
    5. Fricatives appear first in postvocalic position.
    6. Increasing use of different features—acquired in this order (Menyuk, 1968); but features do not generalize to all situations when first acquired (Moskowitz, 1970):
        a. nasal
        b. grave
        c. voice
        d. diffuse
        e. continuant
        f. strident
    7. Must allow for individual variation and the fact that acquisition is gradual (Ferguson and Farwell, 1975; Olmsted, 1971).

C. Phonological Processes (after Ingram, 1976*)
    1. *Syllable Structure Processes*
        a. *Reduplication*
            A syllable of a word is repeated. This occurs most commonly in Stage II,

* From David Ingram, *Phonological Disability in Children*, Elsevier-North Holland Publishing Company. By permission of David Ingram and Edward Arnold (Publishers) Ltd., London, England, Copyright © 1976.

Phonology of the First 50 Words. Use of the process varies among children. Types include

(1)	Complete reduplication of the syllable.	away [ba ba] byebye [baba] daddy [dada]
(2)	Partial reduplication, ending in /i/ (diminutive).	blanket [babi]
(3)	The process may be used productively.	hi [haidi] up [api] no [nodi]
(4)	The process may be related to the child's ability to produce final consonants which might otherwise be deleted.	dog [da] dog [daga]

b. **Unstressed Syllable Deletion** (NPA process)

The unstressed syllable of adult words with more than one syllable is deleted. The following stages may characterize the child's speech until he or she is 4 years old or older.

Stage 1
Only *monosyllabic words* are produced. This is typical of the Phonology of the First 50 Words.

pocket [bat] 1-0
apple [æp] 1-0
blanket [ba] 1-3

Stage 2
Two-syllable words are now produced.

Robbie [wabi:] 2-2, 2-3

(a) Initial unstressed syllables are reduced

away [we:] 2-2, 2-3

(b) All unstressed syllables in trisyllable words are reduced.

Stage 3
Initial unstressed syllables are still reduced, but medial syllables now occur.

tomato [ma:do] 2-2, 2-3
television [dɛwi:bu:n] 2-2, 2-3

Stage 4
(a) Initial unstressed syllables appear now in bisyllable words, but not so much in trisyllable words.

away [we:] [wei] 2-2
    [əwe:] [we:] 2-3
    [əwei] 2-4

banana [ba:nə] 2-2
     [ba:nə] 2-8
     [bəna:nə] 3-1

(b) At onset of Stage 4, the initial unstressed syllables may take on a *single phonetic shape*.

attach [ri:tæk] 3-6, 3-11
arrange [rireɪnz]
disturb [ristə:v]
elastic [ri:læstɪk]

Stage 5
Adult articulation is now used.

c.   **Final Consonant Deletion** (NPA process)

Final consonants tend to be   ball [ba]
deleted, especially in CVC   there [dɛi]
syllables. A common process early
in this period (Stage III, Phonology
of the Simple Morpheme), it
ceases to operate between 1½ and
3 years. Renfrew (1966) posits 10
stages in the appearance of final
consonants for children with
delayed speech development.

Stage	*Description*
1	No final singleton consonants or final clusters.
2	All consonants except /θ/ and /r/ may be used consistently in initial position and occasionally in the medial position (Stage 2 may not be reached until after Stage 4 if speech services are not provided).
3	Two-syllable words are correctly articulated if neither clusters nor *final consonants* are required, e.g., "coffee" will be correctly articulated, but "blanket" may yield [bækə]. When attempting to imitate a word with a final consonant, two syllables are produced, e.g., "dog" [dɔgə], "bus [bʌ-s].
4	Nasal consonants only are used at the ends of words where appropriate; /m/ is used correctly as a final, but /n/ and /ŋ/ vary.
5	Nasal finals are all used consistently and appropriately; /l/ finals and clusters are used and attempts are made at /r/ clusters.
6	Glottal stops are used for all final stops; /r/ and /θ/ are correctly articulated initially and medially.
7	In the final position /p/ and /b/, and /d/ are used consistently and appropriately; glottal stops are still used for /k/, /g/, and /t/, but the length of the vowel preceding the stop indicates which of the three stops was intended.
8	Final /t/ is used consistently and appropriately; sometimes several attempts are made at fricative finals before the correct one is selected.
9	All final consonants, including fricatives, are used consistently and appropriately, except /k/ and /g/.
10	Articulation is normal.

d.   **Cluster Reduction Processes** (NPA process)

Consonant clusters usually are simplified by deletion of one member, usually the marked consonant. Whether the marked or the unmarked consonant is deleted, the following stages (1 through 4) generally occur for each cluster type.

Stage 1

The entire cluster is deleted. This may not be a widespread stage.

This stage is early in development and is affected by Deletion of Final Consonants.

(examples from French)

brouette [ɔɛt] 2-0
crayon [ijon] 2-0
gris [i] 2-0

Stage 2

Clusters are reduced to one member. This is the most common and longest lasting stage.

(1) *Deletion of the Marked Cluster Member*
Types of clusters:

Cluster Type I:	/s/ + consonant—delete /s/	Initial clusters: stop [tʰɑp] 2-8 small [mɑl] 2-4 slide [lɑɪd] 2-7 Final clusters: desk [dɛk] 2-8
Cluster Type II:	stop + liquid—delete liquid	Initial clusters: clock [gɔk] 2-2 bring [biŋ] 2-5 Final clusters: milk [mik] 2-2
Cluster Type III:	fricative + liquid/glide—delete liquid/glide	from [fɔm] 2-10
Cluster Type IV: Substage 1: Substage 2:	nasal + obstruent— Delete nasal. Delete stop if voiced (although the nasal tends to be deleted).	bump [bʌp] 2-2 round [daʊn] 2-2 mend [mɛn] 2-2

(2) *Deletion of the Unmarked Cluster Member*
Less common process; operation for a briefer period if at all.

Cluster Type I:	/s/ + consonant—delete consonant	stop [sɔp] 3-0
Cluster Type II:	stop + liquid—delete stop	trolley [lɔli:] 2-2
Cluster Type III:	fricative + liquid/glide—delete fricative	three [li:] 2-5

(See also the two Assimilation processes affecting liquid clusters, Weakening of Stops, and Labial Assimilation.)

Stage 3

Clusters begin, but they are not yet correct. Most often substitution of one of the members occurs, but the Stage 2 process reducing the cluster to one member still operates.

Processes that separate cluster members to maintain a CVCV

r→l bread [blɛd] 2-7
r→w brown [bwaʊn] 2-6
l→w sleep [fwip] 3-0

syllable structure. These processes are less common.
(1) Vowel insertion (epenthesis). bread [bərɛd] 2-6
(2) Migration of a member. play [bəleɪ] 2-6

blue [bu:l] 2-6

During stage 3, the above
processes vary with correct
articulation.

bread [bɛd]
[brɛd] 2-6
[blɛd]
[blɛd] 2-7
[brɛd]

Stage 4
Correct production of the cluster dominates (90 percent).

2. *Assimilation Processes*
Assimilation sound changes are processes in which a sound in a word becomes similar to or is influenced by another sound in a word (or in the special case of Final Consonant Devoicing, by the silence at the end of a word). The influencing sound may be adjacent to the affected sound, i.e., *contiguous,* or it may be further away, i.e., *noncontiguous.* The influencing sound may *follow* the affected sound, i.e., *regressive assimilation,* or the influencing sound may *precede* the affected sound, i.e., *progressive assimilation.* Including the three special subtypes of Contiguous Assimilation *Between* Consonants (i.e., reciprocal affects), five types of assimilation processes may be observed.
a. Contiguous: Assimilation Between Consonants (C ⇄ C) (the arrow points to the "victim" of the assimilation process).
(1) Weakening of stops.
(2) Labial assimilation.
(3) Devoicing of final consonants.
b. Contiguous: Regressive Assimilation (C←V, V←C).
c. Contiguous: Progressive Assimilation (C→V, V→C).
d. Noncontiguous: Regressive Assimilation (C ⇠ C, V ⇠ V).
e. Noncontiguous: Progressive Assimilation (C ⇢ C, V ⇢ V).

Each of these five types is described in the following pages.
a. *Contiguous Assimilation Between Consonants*
(1) *Weakening of stops* (also   truck [gək] 1-9
under Cluster Reduction,   [gək] 1-10
Stage 2). With the onset of a   [kək] 1-10
liquid, the stop in a   [fək] 2-0
stop-liquid cluster, weakens,   [frək] 2-0
most frequently to the
fricative /f/.
(2) *Labial assimilation* (also   tree [fwi] 2-3, 2-4
under Cluster Reduction,   throw [fo] 2-3, 2-4
Stage 2). The first segment to sweet [fwi] 2-3, 2-4
appear for the liquid in
clusters is generally the glide
/w/. The weakening of the
stop to /f/ may be
assimilation to the labiality of

the /w/ as well as loss of closure.

(3) *Devoicing of final consonants.* Final consonants are devoiced, as an assimilation to the silence at the end of the word. This process becomes effective only after *Deletion of Final Consonants* no longer obtains.

Substage 1:	Final consonants are devoiced.	mud [mat] 1-10 nose [nus]
Substage 2:	Vowels before voiced final consonants are lengthened, but the final consonants are devoiced.	mud [ma·t] nose [nu·s]
Substage 3:	Vowels before voiced final consonants are lengthened, but now the final consonants are voiced.	mud [ma·d] nose [nu·z]

b. *Contiguous: Regressive Assimilation* (more common than Progressive Assimilation)

(1) *C←V:* A *consonant* is determined by the vowels *following* it.

(a) Early in the acquisition process labial sounds are not produced before a front vowel.

(b) The assimilation process may be related to vowels height, i.e., a labial may not appear before a low vowel.

    baby [dɪdɪ]
    dog [ba]

(c) /n/, /t/, and /d/ become velars when preceding a /u/ which has resulted from the Vocalization of a Syllabic Consonant (/l/) (see Substitution Processes).

    pedal [bɛgu] 2-2
    beetle [bigu] 2-2
    bottle [bɔgu] 2-2

(d) Voicing of consonants followed by a vowel.

    pocket [bat]
    push [bus]
    pie [ba]
    toe [du] 1-9
    cap [dap] 1-10
    soup [zup] 1-9

(2) *V←C:* the child's *vowel* is determined by the *consonant* following it.

(a) Vowel lengthening before a voiced consonant.

(b) Nasalization of vowels before nasal consonants. This is a common assimilation.

    friend [frɛ̃]
    dream [drĩ]
    green [grĩ]

(c) Vowel raising,

    neck [nik] 1-9

depending on following   cake [kɪk] 1-9
consonant, e.g., a
midvowel is raised if
followed by /k/.

    c. *Contiguous: Progressive Assimilation* (less common than Regressive Assimilation)

        (1)   *C→V:* A vowel is affected by   Bild [bü] 0-9, 0-10
the *preceding* consonant,
e.g., the lip rounding of the
/b/ is assimilated to the
following vowel.

        (2)   *V→C:* A consonant is   soap [ok]
affected by the *preceding*
vowel, e.g., the back
consonant /k/ is substituted
when preceded by the back
vowel /o/.

    d. *Noncontiguous:* **Regressive Assimilation** (NPA process)

        (1) ˙ *C⤆V̆C:* Consonants are affected by *following* consonants although a vowel comes between them. The following processes are common in the early part of *Phonology of Simple Morphemes*.

            (a)   Alveolar consonants are   talk [kuk]
affected by following   dog [gɔk]
velars, also called: Back   take [kek]
Assimilation; Velar
Harmony.

            (b)   Labial consonants may   knife [mɑɪp]
affect preceding   table [bebu]
consonants.

        (2)   *V⤆CV:* A vowel assimilates to   Handschuh [hadʒu] 1-10
a following vowel (may   [haudʒu] 1-11
occur even after appropriate   Hildegard [hɪta]
vowels have been used).   [hata] 1-11

    e. *Noncontiguous:* **Progressive Assimilation** (NPA process)

        (1)   *C⤆V̆C:* Consonants are affected by *preceding* consonants although a vowel comes between them.

            (a)   Alveolar consonants are   squat [gɔp]
affected by preceding   twice [d̥aif]
labials.

            (b)   Continuants are   noisy [nɔːni]
affected by preceding   smell [mɛn]
nasals (operates only   nice [nait]
occasionally, i.e., not in   smith [mit]
all instances in the same
time period—note
instances in examples).

        (2)   *V⤇CV:* A vowel assimilates to   Loscher [loko] 1-11
a preceding vowel.   apple ['aba] 1-5
                                  ['apa] 1-8

3. *Substitution Processes*

In addition to substitutions due to assimilation processes, certain sounds tend to replace other sounds at different times in the normal acquisition process.

These assumedly simplified replacements generally involve change of manner or place features, but not both. For ease of reference, all substitution processes are listed by the sound class they affect (in developmental order), with outline subdivisions (a, b, c, etc.) left intact.

Processes Affecting Vowels

a. *Vowel Neutralization*
    The most common process for
    vowels (and the only one
    presented here). Vowels are
    reduced to /ə/ or /a/.

    bed [tət]
    teeth [təf]
    basket [səkə]
    boat [tap]

Processes Affecting Nasals

b. *Fronting of Nasals*
    /ŋ/ is replaced by /n/.
c. *Denasalization*
    Nasals are replaced by
    homorganic stops.

    broom [bub] 1-10
    spoon [bud] 1-10
    jam [dab] 1-10
    rain [wud] 1-10

Processes Affecting Glides

d. *Frication of Glides*
    Glides are replaced by available
    fricatives. Glides generally appear
    early, therefore this process is not
    widespread.

    yard [zɑ·d] 2-0
    yellow [zu·wa] 1-11
    wheel [vio] 2-0
    watch [vatʃ] 2-1
    If /h/ is considered a glide:
    house [sɑʊs] 2-4
    hair [sɑɪr] 2-4

Processes Affecting Stops

e. **Velar Fronting** (NPA process)
    /k/ and /g/ are replaced by /t/ and /d/ (common occurrence in young
    children).
    (1) Operates in *all* instances of
         the sound.
    (2) Operates only in *initial* or
         final positions.

    kitty [dɪti] 1-5
    get down [dɪdən] 1-5
    book [but] 1-5
    dog [dɔdi] 1-5
    cake [teik] 2-0
    coat [toʊt] 2-0

Processes Affecting Fricatives and Affricates

f. **Stopping of Fricatives and
    Affricates** (NPA process)
    Fricatives and affricates are
    replaced by homorganic stops.
    Dissolution of the process occurs
    in several stages.

    safe [deif]
    this [dit]
    chair [d̥e]

    Stage 1
    Fricatives and affricates generally
    are omitted or the words used by

    /f/→ø 1-4
    /θ/→ø

the child do not tend to contain them.	/z/→ø /tʃ/→ø

Stage 2

Stopping is used for most or all fricatives and affricates; if fricatives and affricates occur, the form of production often varies.	/f/→/w/ 2-2, 2-5 /θ/→/d/ /z/→/d/ /tʃ/→/d/

Stage 3

Stopping begins to drop out. Many fricatives now appear as continuant sounds (occasionally as a liquid or a glide).	/f/→/f/ /θ/→/t/, /ts/, /s/ /z/→/r/ /tʃ/→/ts/

Stage 4

Most fricatives are correctly produced; /ʒ/, /ð/, and /z/ may still be misarticulated.	/f/→/f/ 2-4 2-6 /s/→/s/ /ð/→/ð/, /d/ /θ/→/θ/, /t/

Stage 5
adult articulation is achieved.

g. **Fronting of Palatals** (NPA process)

Palatals /ʃ/, /ʒ/, /tʃ/, and /dʒ/ are replaced by alveolars.	cheese [tˢiːz] 1-5 chalk [tˢɔːk] 2-11 jump [dʒʌmp] 3-0 chair [tˢɛa] 3-0 shoes [suːz] 3-2 John [dzɔn] 3-3 juice [dzuːs] 3-5

Processes Affecting Liquids

h. **Liquid Simplification** (NPA process)
Liquids /l/ and /r/ may be simplified in three stages.

Stage 1

Stopping of /l/	lady [deidiː] 2-2 light [dait] 2-2
/r/ replaced by /d/	rain [deɪn] 2-2 rat [dæt] 2-3

Stage 2
Most common stage; lasts longer than other stages.

/l/ replaced by /w/ or /j/	lie [jal] 1-11 leaf [ji] light [waɪt] 1-9 lunch [wantʃ] 2-5
/r/ replaced by /w/	rock [wak] 2-5 rabbit [wædæt] 1-9

Stage 3

One liquid is used in place of the other.	ride [laɪd] 2-5
	round [laʊn] 2-5

Processes Affecting Syllabic Nasals and Liquids

i. *Vocalization of Syllabic Consonants*
A syllabic element, /r/, /l/, /m/, /n/ may be replaced by a vowel.

Stage 1

The substituted vowel may be *totally* assimilated to the preceding vowel.	flower [fawa] 1-1
	hammer [hama] 1-1
	table [dabu] 1-11
	bottom [bawa] 1-11
	pudding [budu] 1-11

Stage 2

The substituted vowel is not totally assimilated to the preceding vowel. Tendency for sound to become [ʊ], [ə] or [a] at first; later [o]. Change in the vowel quality may also occur.	cracker [kaku] 1-7
	flower [favo] 1-9
	open [apo] 1-11
	apple [abu] 1-7
	[apo] 1-9

Stage 3

Syllabics are acquired.

**4-0 to 7-0.
Stage IV:
Completion of the
Phonetic Inventory**

The phonetic inventory becomes complete, including fricatives and affricates, by 7 to 8 years—but the child still has difficulty with longer words (some simplifying processes still operating) (Ingram, 1976).

thermometer	[θəmanəbr̩]
	[θr̩manətr̩]
	[θəmpətu]
	[θijamətr̩]

Morphophonemic development also begins to occur for some structures. For plural allomorphs, for example, [s] and [z] are developed, but not [əz] (Ingram, 1976; Berko, 1958).

**7-0 to 12-0.
Stage V:
Morphophonemic
Development**

Morphophonemic (phonological changes that result when one morpheme is added to another) development now includes growth of words with complex morphophonemic structure (Ingram, 1976; Berko, 1958; Atkinson-King, 1973).

A. Vowel Alternations (vowel shift rule):
devine→divinity
explain→explanation
serene→serenity

B. Pluralization:
use of [əz] following /s/, /z/, /dʒ], /tʃ/, /ʃ/, and /ʒ/

C. Stress Alterations:
rédhead (compound)
red head (phrase)

12 to 16.
Stage VI:
Spelling

Mastery of spelling.

APPENDIX B

Answers to the Review and
Discussion Questions

AP

Review and Discussion Questions, page 31

5. a. The plural morpheme, /s/, was only assumed in the gloss
   b. The clinician was undecided about the correct gloss; however, the best guess is that the child meant to say "the."
   c. The clinician was unsure that the child meant to say "get"—this word, accordingly, would not be chosen for coding.
6. Each word (a–d) would be entered in the gloss box exactly as written; "snowsuit" would be treated as a two-syllable word.
7. a. [faɪr]
   b. [fɝ]
   c. [brʌðɚ]
8. a. [kɝt]
   b. [mʌðɚ]
   c. dɑɪk]
   d. [rɛd]
9. a. [kʌt]
   b. [mʌðə]
   c. [dɑk]
   d. The clinician was unsure of the final segment—this word would not be chosen for coding.

Review and Discussion Questions, page 44

1. Only the *first* occurrence of a word is coded unless the clinician thinks that the word should not be coded because of a glossing or transcription problem.
2.

	Sheet	Column	Row
a.	B	1	/g/
b.	C	3	/z/
c.	B	3	/k/
d.	B	5	/t/
e.	A	6	/w/
f.	C	4	/s/
g.	C	5	/z/
h.	C	1	/h/
i.	B	6	/p/

3. Look it up in Kenyon and Knott's *A Pronouncing Dictionary of American English.*

Review and Discussion Questions, page 49

1. In the interests of standardization consistency, data are taken only from the Coding Sheets.
2. No, the information on the Summary Sheet provides only an overview of the child's phonetic inventory and use of natural processes. As such, Summary Sheet data are useful for monitoring a child's progress and other descriptive needs. For an "in-depth" look at the child's *phonological* system, additional analyses are needed.

Blan

NPA CODING SHEET

Shriberg and Kwiatkowski
John Wiley & Sons   Copyright 1980 NPA

Child _____ DOB _____
Sampling _____ Age _____
Date _____ Analysis _____
Clinician _____ Date _____

Coding Sheet: □ C □ Fricatives; Affricates
Page No. _____

Total Words Entered _____

Sounds: [h, f, v, θ, ð, s, z, ʃ, ʒ, tʃ, dʒ]

Sound	1 CV			2 VC			3 CVC			4 Cⁿ V(C)			5 (C) VCⁿ			6 Two-Syllable			7 Three⁺ Syllable		
	Gloss	Trans.	Code	Gloss	Trans.	Code	Gloss	Trans.	Code	Gloss	Trans.	Code	Gloss	Trans.	Code	Gloss	Trans.	Code	Gloss	Trans.	Code
h																					
f																					
v																					
θ																					
ð																					
s																					
z																					
ʃ																					
ʒ																					
tʃ																					
dʒ																					

NPA SUMMARY SHEET

Shriberg and Kwiatkowski
John Wiley & Sons   Copyright 1980 NPA

Child _____ DOB _____
Sampling _____ Age _____
Date _____ Analysis _____
Clinician _____ Date _____

PROCESS SYMBOLS

✓ Always Occurs
∅ Sometimes Occurs
O Never Occurs
– No Data Available

Total Words
Entered _____
(A + B + C) _____

Phonetic Inventory	m	n	ŋ	w	j	p	b	t	d	k	g	h	f	v	θ	ð	s	z	ʃ	ʒ	tʃ	dʒ	l	r

Correct Anywhere →
Appears Anywhere →
Glossed Never Correct →
Never Appears →
Never Glossed; Never Appears →

1 Final Consonant Deletion →

2 Velar Fronting — Initial → / Final →

3 Stopping — Initial → / Final →

4 Palatal Fronting — Initial → / Final →

5 Liquid Simplification

6 Progressive Assimilations / Regressive Assimilations

NPA CODING SHEET

Shriberg and Kwiatkowski
John Wiley & Sons   Copyright 1980 NPA

Child _____ DOB _____
Sampling _____ Age _____
Date _____ Analysis _____
Clinician _____ Date _____

Coding Sheet: [C] Fricatives; Affricates
Page No. _____
Total Words Entered _____
Sounds : [h, f, v, θ, ð, s, z, ʒ, ʃ, tʃ, dʒ]

1 CV **2** VC **3** VC CVC C^n V(C) (C) VC^n **4** **5** **6** Two-Syllable **7** Three⁺ Syllable

Sounds: h, f, v, θ, ð, s, z, ʃ, ʒ, tʃ, dʒ

Columns: Gloss | Trans. | Code

NPA SUMMARY SHEET

Shriberg and Kwiatkowski
John Wiley & Sons   Copyright 1980 NPA

Child _____   DOB _____
Sampling _____   Age _____
Date _____   Analysis ____
Clinician _____   Date _____

Total Words Entered (A+B+C) _____

	m	n	ŋ	w	j	p	b	t	d	k	g	h	f	v	θ	ð	s	z	ʃ	ʒ	tʃ	dʒ	l	r
Phonetic Inventory																								
Correct Anywhere →																								
Appears Anywhere →																								
Glossed Never Correct; Never Appears →																								
Never Glossed; Never Appears →																								
1 Final Consonant Deletion →																								